Positive Peer Culture

Positive Peer Culture

Second Edition

Harry H. Vorrath
Larry K. Brendtro

ALDINE TRANSACTION
A Division of Transaction Publishers
New Brunswick (U.S.A.) and London (U.K.)

Second paperback printing 2007

This book is printed on acid-free paper that meets the American National Standard for Permanence of Paper for Printed Library Materials.

Library of Congress Catalog Number: 84-21570
ISBN: 978-0-202-36038-6
Printed in the United States of America

Library of Congress Cataloging-in-Publication Data

Vorrath, Harry H.
    Positive Peer Culture.
    (Modern applications of social work)
    Bibliography: p.
    1. Adolescence. 2. Small groups. 3. Groups relations training.
    4. Adolescent psychology. I. Brendtro, Larry K. II. Title.
    III. Series.

HQ796.V685   1985   305.2'35   84-21570
ISBN 0-202-36037-7
ISBN 0-202-36038-5 (pbk.)

This work is dedicated to the true founders of Positive Peer Culture, those strong and noble young people who comprehend the power of caring.

CONTENTS

FOREWORD

Harry H. Vorrath
Larry K. Brendtro

The central position of this book is that young people can develop self-worth, significance, dignity, and responsibility only as they become committed to the positive values of helping and caring for others. While this philosophy appears to be missing in many of today's education and treatment programs, the general concept has a rich place in history. Shakespeare observed that "It is one of the most beautiful compensations of this life that no man can sincerely help another without helping himself." Most major religions extol the virtue of service to others. An ancient Hindu proverb advises "Help thy brother's boat across, and lo, thine own has reached the shore." The Christian, Jewish, and Moslem faiths all stress the value of extending kindness to others, even if they are strangers.

In the 1800s, the American educational philosopher, Horace Mann, argued that childhood should be an apprenticeship in responsibility, preparing children for the moral attitudes of self-government and service to others. During the same period, a pioneer in the work with troubled youth, S. D. Brooks, recognized their great potential for service. As superintendent of a New York training school in the mid-nineteenth century, his enthusiasm was unbounded as he declared, "The very qualities of sagacity and daring which formerly rendered them a terror to the community will push them forward in their new career of virtue, honor, and usefulness."

However, the optimism of the 1800s gave way to the reality of the urbanized, industrialized twentieth century. Social critics marked the depersonalization of life, the failures of our societal institutions, and the emptiness of childhood and adolescence. The anthropologist Benedict [1] observed that contemporary society does not provide meaningful role opportunities for youth; rather, it prevents them from assuming adult responsibilities and then blames youth for their irresponsibility and belligerence.

When the first edition of *Positive Peer Culture* was written in the early

1970s, young people in our society were seen by many as the "me generation." It was as if the Jeffersonian concept of "life, liberty, and the pursuit of happiness" had been mutated to mean freedom to "do one's own thing" and "look out for number one" in a climate of consumption and indifference to social responsibility. Sadly, many of our schools and treatment institutions, and even our theories of human behavior, still support this self-centered irresponsibility.

In a most penetrating analysis of this phenomenon, Michael and Lise Wallach [10] of Duke University indict the major theories of human psychology as promoting selfishness.

> There is currently in our society an enormous emphasis on the self . . . narcissism, self-concern and preoccupation with "me". . . . A surprisingly broad and influential range of psychological theory turns out to legitimatize selfishness. Although this is usually far from what is intended, support is lent by academic thinkers as well as clinicians, by Freudians as well as anti-Freudians, by behaviorists as well as contenders against behaviorism, and by psychologists who investigate altruism as by those who deny its existence [p. ix].

They observed that the classic psychoanalytic position reduces human behavior to innate drives that are satisfied by the pleasure principle; self-sacrifice, once seen as a virtue, is presumed to be motivated by neurotic guilt. The behaviorist sees altruism as a special case of self-reinforcement where individuals engage in efforts on behalf of others in order to promote themselves. Even humanistic psychologists are caught in this "error of egoism" by assuming that the most worthy human goal is the quest for self-expression.

In this kind of cynical, psychological world view, there is no real place for gratitude since no one is really genuinely concerned. Even if you really wanted to help someone else, the ultimate basis of your motivation is what you expect to gain by doing so. In such a climate, work that contributes to the welfare of others is devalued. Commitment to a spouse in marriage is undermined, and sacrifices for one's children or parents are suspect because they may interfere with self-expression and freedom. Concluding that therapy need not be cast only in forms that encourage selfishness, the Wallachs call for alternatives. They note a scattered but powerful alternative view within psychology. Allport, Mowrer, Adler, and Frankel all support the idea that it is essential for a person to step outside of himself to care for other humans without thought of return, and such acts of service can heal psychological wounds. Menninger observes that major religions identify self-centeredness as the central human problem and love as the means of overcoming it—self-preoccupation is displaced by assuming responsibility beyond one's self.

The field of education has also been preoccupied with the self to the detriment of building a climate of cooperation. Johnson and Johnson [7] note that the three major formats for learning are cooperation, competition, and individualization. Competition is the dominant pattern in regular classrooms as student is pitted against student in a struggle of educational fitness. Rejecting competition, special educators turn instead to precisely measured individual objectives; but even as they seek to meet the needs of the individual child, they often fail to address the goal of developing caring interpersonal behaviors. As in psychology, there are hopeful signs of a course correction from the "self-ish" toward the interpersonal approach that seeks to build communities of caring. This is seen in the renewed interest in topics such as peer tutoring or counseling [6], social skill instruction [4], the social psychology of learning [9], and moral and value development [8].

The Carnegie Foundation studies of the problems and needs of youth in this nation emphasize the crucial importance of involving young people in helping others. Noting that a vast industry serves youth with schooling, entertainment, and goods of all kinds, our society offers limited opportunities for the young themselves to be of service to others [3]. Perhaps high technology economies do not have the capacity of absorbing a mass of youth in formal employment roles; nevertheless, widespread opportunities for volunteer service exist by involving young people in helping one another and in meeting other needs that exist in every community. In a major study of American high schools, the Carnegie Foundation called for all of the nation's secondary schools to establish involvement in some volunteer service activity as a requirement for high school graduation [2].

The authors are most encouraged by recent trends in the fields of education and treatment that show promise of directing young people away from narcissism and conflict toward a spirit of concern and service for others. It is our sincere hope that this book can make a contribution in this regard. As with our earlier edition, we strive insofar as possible to maintain a simplicity of style of presentation, directing our remarks to the practitioner. However, this is not to say that developing positive caring cultures of young people is a simple process. Therefore, we have felt it important to add material to this edition that seeks to clarify some of the misunderstandings that have arisen as various persons have sought to implement this methodology. Other additions to this revision include a new chapter on the development of positive peer culture in school settings and a discussion of programs for creating service-learning programs that generalize helping beyond the peer group to the community. In the final chapter, we discuss issues related to evaluation and quality control in peer-group programs and provide an overview of the literature concerning the impact of positive peer culture.

Young people who populate our nation's schools and youth institutions are in desperate need of an antidote to the narcissism, malaise, and antisocial life-styles that have become so prevalent. As Gallup and Poling [5] conclude from their survey of contemporary youth, the emerging generation is more than hinting, now almost screaming, to be used in some demanding cause. This book seeks to provide a way of meeting this cry of youth.

NOTES

[1] R. Benedict, "Continuities and Discontinuities in Cultural Conditioning," *Psychiatry* 1 (1938): 161–167.

[2] E. L. Boyer, *High School: A Report on Secondary Education in America*, Report of the Carnegie Council on Policy Studies in Higher Education (New York: Harper & Row, 1983).

[3] The Carnegie Foundation, *Giving Youth a Better Chance*, Report of the Carnegie Council on Policy Studies in Higher Education (San Francisco: Jossey-Bass, 1979).

[4] G. Cartledge and J. Milburn, *Teaching Social Skills to Children* (New York: Pergamon, 1980).

[5] G. Gallup and D. Poling, *The Search for America's Faith* (Nashville: Abingdon, 1980).

[6] J. Jenkins and L. Jenkins, "Cross Age and Peer Tutoring: Help for Children with Learning Problems" (Reston, Va: Council for Exceptional Children, 1981).

[7] D. Johnson and R. Johnson, *Learning Together and Alone: Cooperation, Competition, and Individualization* (Englewood Cliffs, N.J.: Prentice-Hall, 1975).

[8] A. Lockwood, "The Effects of Values Clarification and Moral Development Curricula on School-Aged Subjects: A Critical Review of Research," *Review of Educational Research* 48 (1978): 325–364.

[9] J. H. McMillan, ed., *The Social Psychology of School Learning* (New York: Academic Press, Inc., 1980).

[10] M. A. Wallach and L. Wallach, *Psychology's Sanction for Selfishness: The Error of Egoism in Theory and Therapy* (San Francisco: W. H. Freeman, 1983).

ACKNOWLEDGMENTS

The many contributions of scores of colleagues and young people to the development of Positive Peer Culture make true acknowledgment an impossibility. We owe debts of gratitude to those who preceded us in work with youth. We are grateful to the untiring efforts of staff in the various Positive Peer Culture programs throughout the United States and abroad.

FROM ONE DELINQUENT
TO ANOTHER

> Jeff and Brad were friends who were referred by a juvenile court to Positive Peer Culture (PPC) programs in separate residential schools.

Dear Jeff,

I got your letter today. Hey I'm sorry I haven't dropped you a line. After I read your letter I saw you weren't doing so good. Look Jeff, you can't keep playing games, you have to get down to business and start working on your problems. Things are hard I know because I'm going through the same thing. But I have a positive attitude. Jeff this is the best thing that could have happened for the both of us. Listen man, PPC is a second chance, take advantage of it.

You know when I first came I had them all fooled. At least I thought I did. I told the group I had my stuff together and I wasn't going to mess up. But the one person I didn't fool was myself. For 2 months I was perfect I mean I was an angel. Thought I would be out in a month or so. But hell no, they were onto my crap, they knew I was putting on a front. Once they had to write a report to court. They said I was fronting. I denied it up and down. Well, I went home for Thanksgiving and Christmas. I was up to the same old bull for Thanksgiving but by Christmas it was different. You remember Murray and some of the guys we used to be tight with. Well they came around and we had a good time but I noticed something. Jeff, they are all big fronts. I mean it man. I couldn't believe it but that's how it is and that's the way we are. There's one difference though we have a chance to change. After seeing all this I said no more playing around. I have to get it together and Jeff that's just what I'm doing. In school I pulled an A and three Bs and I also got a physical fitness award in gym. I was really proud of myself. You know how I used to be. I spent more time playing pinball than I spent in school.

Look Jeff, if I can do it then you can do it. And if you are the Jeff I used to know then you're going to pull through. Well I guess there isn't much more I can say. You take care and when we get out we're still going to be tight, OK? Write back.

Be cool,
Brad

INTRODUCTION

What Is Positive Peer Culture?

- A student hurls a book across the room, laughs, and blurts out a remark designed to disrupt the class. Before the teacher can respond, other students in the room confront the offender for being "inconsiderate" and tell him to "check" himself. The youth, having received no peer support for his actions, slumps quietly into his seat. The teacher resumes her instruction without having said one word about the behavior problem.

- The metropolitan transit authority announced its intention of discontinuing cross-town bus service for junior high school students after repeated incidents of serious vandalism. Ten students from the school's peer-leadership program offered to resolve the problem. They contacted various students who rode the buses, found out what had happened, and asked for a commitment for no further destruction. Thus confronted by their influential peers, the students willingly cooperated in the elimination of further problems on these buses.

- A group home for troubled girls had severe drug abuse problems. The result of the many attempts to suppress the activity was a cold war between staff and youth. Suspicion, searches, and restriction became commonplace. That was a year ago. Now staff members no longer police students for drugs, and the climate of intrigue is gone. As a new girl enters, her peers confiscate any drugs she may have and tell her, "We don't have to use dope around here." Drug problems are dealt with openly in a helpful, matter-of-fact way. Group members state with strong conviction that when a person has good feelings about herself she no longer needs to get high on drugs.

- In a residential treatment center for court-committed youth, a new student suggests to others that he is planning to run away. Instead of finding partners in truancy, he encounters a totally unexpected peer response. "Listen, running isn't where it's at. That's just a copout. You have to face things. We're not going to let you mess over yourself; if we have to stay up all night and put our mattresses in front of your door to make sure you're still here in the morning, we will. But we really don't like to sleep on the floor, guarding you like you're a child. You're man enough to take care of yourself!"

■ Students from an alternative school for troubled youth volunteered their services to the community by chopping wood for the elderly, repainting playground equipment for neighborhood children, and assisting in a Special Olympics for the handicapped.

What is happening in these situations? In each, young people are part of a program called Positive Peer Culture (hereafter, PPC).

PPC departs decisively from traditional approaches and charts a new course in the fields of education and treatment. A comprehensive strategy for dealing with the problems of youth, PPC teaches students to assume responsibility for helping one another.

Young people are profoundly influenced by associations with their peers. Too often the peer group has been viewed only as a liability; too seldom has it been seen as a resource. Just as peer group influence can foster problems, so also can the peer process be used to solve problems.

PPC is not a new brand of group therapy that has just appeared on the market. Nor is PPC "something extra" that can be added to an existing program, as one might attach accessories to an automobile. Instead, *PPC is a total system for building positive youth subcultures.*

Although first developed for delinquent youth, PPC now is being employed in a wide range of settings. Schools, community programs, juvenile courts, group homes, and other childcare facilities have found PPC to be a clear and viable alternative to existing programs.

The history of PPC can be traced to the senior author's experiences at Highfields in the late 1950s. This residential treatment program for delinquent youth was established in a mansion given to the state of New Jersey by Charles A. Lindbergh. There, under the guidance of Lloyd McCorkle, Lovell Bixby, Albert Elias, and others, a peer-oriented treatment model called Guided Group Interaction (GGI) was developed. In this approach, structured peer groups met five times weekly in group counseling sessions, and youth assumed responsibility for one another's behavior outside the group meetings. The program at Highfields received wide attention as an innovative treatment design.* allowing
                                                                Control

*PPC is heavily indebted to contributions made in the field of GGI. Although it diverges considerably from GGI, the format of PPC draws extensively from prior work in this area. The idea of structured group sessions was first introduced in army correctional institutions during World War II by Lloyd McCorkle [3]. After the war, he and F. Lovell Bixby [4] introduced the concept at the Highfields residential treatment center in New Jersey. A more recent application of GGI is seen in the program of halfway houses [2].

Following his experience at Highfields, Harry Vorrath worked with colleagues to employ this model in a variety of community and institutional settings. In response to certain initial problems, the program was modified, expanded, and refined until it reached its present form. The result is a comprehensive and specific treatment methodology, now known as Positive Peer Culture.

Built around groups of nine youth under the guidance of an adult leader, PPC is designed to "turn around" a negative youth subculture and mobilize the power of the peer group in a productive manner. Youth in PPC groups learn how to identify problems and how to work toward their resolution. In group sessions and in day-to-day activities, the goal is to fully involve young people in the helping process.

In contrast to traditional treatment approaches, PPC does not ask whether a person wants to receive help but whether he is willing to give help. As the person gives and becomes of value to others, he increases his own feelings of worthiness and builds a positive self-concept.

PPC does not avoid the challenge of troublesome youth; rebellious and strong-willed individuals, when redirected, have much to contribute. Those who have encountered many difficulties in their own lives are often in the best position to understand the problems of others.

PPC does not seek to impose specific rules but to teach basic values. If there were one rule, it would be that people must care for one another. Caring means wanting what is best for a person. Unfortunately, positive caring behavior is not always popular among youth. In fact, negative, harmful behavior frequently is more acceptable. Therefore, PPC uses specific procedures to foster caring behavior. Once caring becomes fashionable, hurting goes out of style.

PPC has had its most dramatic success to date in turning around schools and institutions that were plagued with severe problems of student unrest and adult–youth conflict. In *Children in Trouble: A National Scandal* [1], a nationwide study of programs for problem youth, the Pulitzer-prize-winning journalist Howard James described the success of PPC in a school for delinquent youth.

> Mr. Vorrath was given the opportunity to prove that his ideas worked with small groups in Kentucky, Washington, D.C., and in scattered spots across the country. The projects were successful. He was able to turn small groups of tough delinquents around. But Mr. Vorrath wanted to try his program at a large institution.
>
> He got his chance in 1968 after things fell apart at a rather average reform school at Red Wing, Minnesota. Youngsters rioted and ran. Mr. Vorrath was called in.
>
> Using a technique that might be described as building a culture of caring, Mr. Vorrath divides the boys into groups [with each member] responsible for all the boys in his group.
>
> His program is built on love—"not the sweet, sugar-coated kind," he adds. "I'm talking about the unselfish love that makes a Marine crawl on his belly into enemy fire to save a wounded buddy."

There can be little doubt that the program works. At Red Wing, I talked to boys sprawled on the lawn playing chess on a warm Sunday afternoon. Others batted a baseball around—all without supervision. The boys learn to help each other stay out of trouble.

Two-, three-, and four-time losers agree that before Mr. Vorrath arrived, they could "con" the staff into letting them go home by pretending to conform to institutional requirements. No attitudinal improvement took place. All this is changing.

There are still important questions to be answered. Will Mr. Vorrath's culture of caring—what one finds in a strong, happy family—last after Mr. Vorrath has moved on to other institutions? Can he teach others to build his culture? And can youngsters so absorb this philosophy of caring deeply for others that they can survive on their own in the harsh, dog-eat-dog world they came from?

[Nevertheless] I was more heartened by what I saw at Red Wing than by anything else going on in large institutions anywhere in America.

Currently, PPC programs are operating in all parts of the country and in a variety of settings.

■ An urban midwestern high school that was beset by riots, police surveillance of hallways, and a high dropout rate is now the scene of positive rapport between students and faculty. The guidance department tells PPC groups about any student who is nearing failure or suspension so that peers may have the opportunity to help him to succeed. Students of diverse cultural and ethnic backgrounds are no longer warring but work together to solve mutual problems.

■ A large state correctional school operates with unlocked doors for the first time in more than a century. The atmosphere is no longer clouded with fear, mistrust, and intimidation. Teachers are now free to teach without being entangled in futile attempts to discipline and control youth.

■ A group of youth, once a street gang that had engaged in dozens of undetected felonies, now works as an adjunct to the juvenile court. Members serve as assistant probation officers and are assigned to help with new offenders. This court, which had had great difficulty in recovering runaway youth, now uses peers to locate truants and "talk them back in" so they may be involved in constructive treatment.

PPC is not a permissive, laissez-faire approach but places considerable demands on youth. Although adults remain in charge, young people have the responsibility for helping one another. They must learn that no one has a right to ignore a person in need, for in the words of George Bernard Shaw: "The worst sin toward our fellow creatures is not to hate them but to be indifferent to them: that's the essence of inhumanity." PPC asks much of youth in the knowledge that people seldom will be more responsible than they are expected to be or more helpful than they are allowed to be.

PPC is a synthesis of several long-known but seldom-utilized principles. While PPC can be related to theories of learning and group processes, it grows not from theory but from practice. PPC was not suddenly invented but has gradually emerged through years of searching for those factors that underlie successful group programs. The procedures that have evolved are those that have survived the tests of time and experience.

Although the basic concepts of PPC can be easily understood, it is no simple matter to produce a truly positive culture of young people. Careful planning and organization are necessary, with attention given to many different variables. An effective program also requires properly trained staff who are committed to the task of developing the positive potentials of youth. This book outlines the ingredients and procedures essential to such a program.

NOTES

[1] Howard James, *Children in Trouble: A National Scandal* (New York: Pocket Books, 1971), pp. 124–126.

[2] Oliver J. Keller, Jr. and Benedict S. Alper, *Halfway Houses: Community Centered Correction and Treatment* (Lexington, Mass.: Heath, 1970).

[3] Lloyd McCorkle, "Group Therapy in Correctional Institutions," *Federal Probation* 13, no. 2 (1949).

[4] Lloyd McCorkle, Albert Elias, and F. Lovell Bixby, *The Highfields Story* (New York: Henry Holt, 1958).

Foundations of
Positive Peer Culture

> How many things, which for our own sake we would never do, do we perform for the sake of our friends.
> —Cicero

THE POWER OF PEERS

In most cultures, the training of children begins in infancy and continues until adolescence, whereupon the individual enters the adult role. Even in primitive cultures, this pattern is common and often includes an initiation ceremony, a "right of passage," to mark the transition from childhood to adulthood.

In modern society, adult status comes many years after adolescence. While a young person achieves physical maturity and wants social independence, he* must remain in a position of dependency. He is compelled to continue in the role of student and is not allowed to compete with adults in the job market. He is out of place in the friendship patterns of adults; he has no legitimate outlet for his newly developed drives; he is not allowed to do the things that adults do for enjoyment and relaxation. Seemingly, society has no role for him, for he is not a child nor is he an adult. So while children "resign" from childhood in their early teens, they do not "enlist" in adulthood until they are fully independent, sometimes as much as a decade later. During this entire period, youth are in a cultural limbo, being neither obedient children nor responsible adults.

*We here use the pronoun he for simplicity. As in the Old Testament where the Hebrew name "Adam" can refer either to the first man or to humankind, so our use of the generic term he refers not to a male but to any human being.

1

Out of their need to be something more than children and to achieve some independence, youth have created their own subculture. Complete with its own values, norms, language, and symbols, the subculture has become so well developed and organized that it spans continents and oceans. The unusual styles of dress and grooming, folk heroes, and slang expressions seem more foreign to the parent who lives under the same roof than to another young person thousands of miles away.

Adults continue in attempts to socialize youth but find they have less and less power, while the youth subculture seems to take an increasingly strong hold. As time goes on, the peer group all but replaces the influence of parents and other adults.

> The need of adolescents to conform to peer group norms and values has often been witnessed by youth workers as well as parents. When one refers to the "tyranny of adolescents" one is expressing an awesome appreciation of the powerful energy and pressures generated by this strange social configuration called the peer group [1].

Adults decry their loss of influence and dream nostalgically of the family of the past where children knew their place and the elders ruled supreme. But it is not possible to turn back the clock to another day when the young person found his peer group among either children or adults. The reality must be accepted as it is: *The peer group has the strongest influence over the values, attitudes, and behavior of most youth.*

This peer influence might be acceptable if young people were able to succeed at operating their private subculture in a manner that did not cause concern among adults. Unfortunately, society is concerned not only with the lower-class ghetto delinquents but also with many peer patterns formed in the suburbs among young people from seemingly favorable backgrounds. Too seldom we find a peer group composed of young people with values, maturity, stability, and judgment necessary to guide one another into happy and productive roles in the broader society. All too often it seems more like a case of the blind leading the blind, while the supposedly sighted adult stands helplessly on the sidelines.

The various responses of adults in authority to the power of the peer culture merit notice.

Conflict: Perhaps the most universal response is the contest for power. With the motto "we'll show them who is boss," adults attempt to instill in the life of the young an obedience that belonged to an earlier time. As controls become restrictive, friction and conflict increase. Adults who feel they are about to lose control frequently send for reinforcements. Parents turn to schools, guidance clinics, and juvenile courts for support. Teachers call for parents to help monitor the cafeteria and for security guards to patrol the hallways. In the end, adults may succeed in applying enough control to impose conformity, but the problems now have gone underground. It is all too easy for the young person to appease the adult with superficial compliance while still remaining basically loyal to different values of his peer group.

Liberation: Another response of adults to the peer group is that of liberation. These adults say: "Go ahead and do your own thing. . . . You are old enough to decide for yourselves." Such adults may be enthusiastic supporters of "how wonderful today's young people are"; still they are often troubled by the recurrent feeling that perhaps youth are not yet able to meet all of the challenges of independence.

Surrender: Adults often surrender to the power of the youth subculture. Here the adult experiences feelings of futility. "There's nothing I can do; they won't listen anymore." The young person is left trying to manage his life while the adult ponders just where his approach went wrong.

Joining the opposition: Another variation in adult response to the peer subculture is enlistment in the opposition. Perhaps uttering the trite slogan, "If you can't beat them, join them," the adult tries to become like the young person. The adult, struggling valiantly to imitate the youth culture (which never allows grownups as real members), is as completely out of place as he is ineffective.

Enlisting the opposition: This is the response of PPC, which assumes that all of the foregoing styles are inadequate ways of dealing with the peer subculture. Even though the peer group is the most potent influence on youth, adults have much to offer to young people. Furthermore, adults should neither become locked in combat with them nor capitulate to them. Therefore, PPC seeks to encompass and win over the peer group.

An analogy comes to mind. The highly developed Japanese art of jujitsu, when mastered, enables even very small persons to deal with powerful adversaries. It is not necessary to be stronger than an opponent, since force need not be met with force. Rather, the adversary's strength and movement are channeled into a different direction to achieve the intended result. In the same way, it is not necessary to overcome the peer group's power; instead, the peer group's action is rechanneled to achieve the intended goal. Here the analogy ends, for our intention is not to defeat young people but to bring forth their potentials.

> Help thy brother's boat across and lo!
> thine own has reached the shore.
> —Hindu proverb

THE REWARDS OF GIVING

In traditional approaches to the problems of youth, adults monopolize the giving of help. In contrast, PPC demands that young people assume the task of giving help among themselves. This notion of helping is, of course, not original; civilized man has long been aware of the benefits that accrue when people are involved in mutual giving. Isaiah expressed this idea nearly 3000 years ago: "They helped every one his neighbor."

Many organizations flourish mainly because they offer individuals opportunities to serve others. Through the Peace Corps, fraternal groups, volunteer hospital auxiliaries, Big Brother and Big Sister organizations, and the numerous other ways, people assume roles of giving. Those who work in education and the helping professions also derive a great deal of personal satisfaction from contributing to the well-being of others.

Throughout all of our "helping" we have not looked closely enough at the effect of help on the receiving individual. Does being the recipient of help really make a person feel positive about himself? Are we somehow maintaining individuals in helpless and dependent roles? *Being helpful* usually has an enhancing effect on one's self-concept; *needing help* and being dependent on others often worsens the erosion of what may already be a weak self-concept.

In order for an individual to feel positive about himself, two conditions must exist. First, he must feel accepted by others. Second, he must feel that he deserves this acceptance. Many traditional approaches concentrate on the first condition and overlook the second.

Being accepted: In the past, we have gone to great lengths to tell the troubled person that he is really not so bad as he thinks, that he is worthy as an individual, that he has many fine qualities, and that we accept him. However, just telling someone he is a fine person and treating him kindly is not enough to make the person view himself positively. The person often thinks we are being nice to him only because we feel sorry for him or perhaps even because we are getting paid to be nice.

Deserving acceptance: Despite how others relate to him, a person may feel he is not worthy of acceptance. He knows that much of his behavior is irresponsible and damaging to himself or others, and further, he does not believe he is really making worthwhile contributions to life. If he is to feel deserving of the acceptance, he must start making positive contributions to others and stop harmful behavior.

Figure 1.1 suggests the effects of PPC and traditional treatment approaches on a negative self-concept. Both PPC and traditional approaches strive to make a person feel accepted. However, in traditional therapy an individual often continues irresponsible behavior, and traditional therapy seldom provides the means for one to be of value to others. In contrast, PPC expects that the person will both stop his irresponsible (hurting) behavior and begin helping others. These are the ingredients of a truly positive self-concept.

Contrary to established notions, one need not conquer all of one's own problems before being able to help solve the problems of others. PPC does

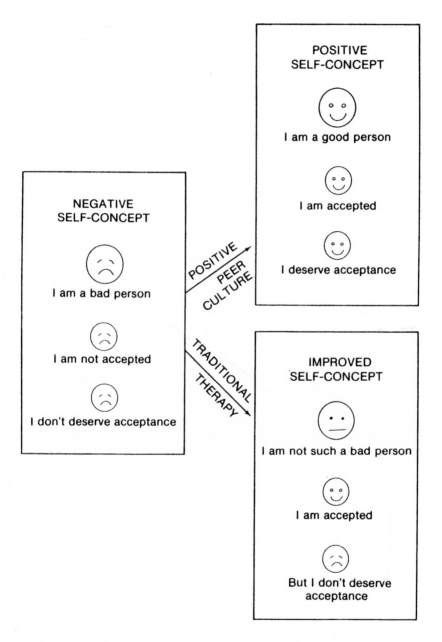

Figure 1.1. Effects of PPC and traditional treatment approaches on negative self-concept.

Service
depression
+
addiction

not wait until the individual can "cure" all of his own hang-ups before it expects him to contribute to others. Rather, the very act of helping others becomes the first decisive step in overcoming one's personal problems. In reaching out to help another a person creates his own proof of worthiness: he is now of value to someone.

It is widely assumed that a primary determinant of success in therapy is that the person be able to ask for help, admitting to his inadequacy and need for assistance. In fact, our experience has indicated that the individual whose approach to us is "Please rehabilitate me" or "I think I need help and I feel you can help me" may be in worse trouble than the one who denies the need for help. Most often such an approach tells us one of two things: (1) this is a weak, helpless, ego-deficient individual who is all too ready to surrender to his own inadequacies, or (2) this is a con artist telling the therapist what somebody seeking help is supposed to say. Neither of these possibilities speaks well for the person's prospects for change.

The young person who tells us "You are not going to get me to change" is not saying he is unwilling to change. In reality, most youth are considerably more receptive to change than are older individuals. What such a person is really saying is that "I am not going to be changed *by you*," a very different situation. Young people do not resist change: They only resist *being changed.*

Rather than hoping the youth will come forth with a "cry for help," PPC asks first that he be willing to offer help to others. While an individual certainly must learn to receive as well as to give help, the balance must be weighted in favor of giving—the only route to true strength, autonomy, and a positive self-concept. In PPC, the entire process of helping others is given highest status. The young person does not have to be *cured* because he is mentally ill, *punished* because he is immoral, or *enlightened* because he is ignorant. Rather, he comes to *help others* and thereby to receive help with his own problems.

> He who helps in the saving of others saves himself as well.
>
> —Hartmann von Aue

THE STRENGTH OF THE REFORMED

The person who has successfully overcome adversity and resolved problems often has great potential for understanding the problems of others and helping them to master similar difficulties. This principle has not found widespread application except in isolated instances, most notably in Alcoholics Anonymous. In this organization, the fight against alcoholism is not waged by professionals trained in the characteristics and treatment of alcoholics; rather, it is the reformed alcoholic who is the core and power of such a program. The most potent influence on the alcoholic is that exerted by another alcoholic. As the reformed individual attacks what he once embraced, he both directs others away from involvement and counteracts his own tendencies to resume such behavior. This powerful treatment concept has been little understood except by those who have directly experienced its impact.*

When working with troublesome youth, we all too often see only their limitations and not their strengths. The traditional mental health view is that behavior problems result from emotional disturbance or mental illness. Since these youth have experienced much conflict, neglect, and rejection, we assume that somehow they were severely damaged and weakened by such experiences. In reality, the tremendous pressures in the lives of these troubled youth have in some respects made them stronger than many "normal" youngsters. What "normal, well-adjusted child" would even dare to simultaneously challenge parents, principals, and police, declaring that no one can tell him what to do? Yet troubled youth frequently show such "strength"; with stubborn determination and at considerable personal risk, they stand up against powerful individuals. Although such behavior may be foolish and even self-destructive, it does show considerable fortitude. Seldom have these troublesome youth been viewed as a potential resource. In PPC negative, rebellious students frequently become the strongest and most positive members of the group. Once the "toughness" is redirected, they can become as strong in providing help as they were in provoking conflict.

[Margin annotation: Deviance → Strength; leadership]

The difficult youth who is beginning to understand his own problems becomes truly an expert in dealing with other youth of similar background. He will acquire considerable knowledge about those in his group, and other members will not find it easy to deceive him. The best expert on defending, excusing, and shifting the blame is the person who himself uses these procedures. Nobody can deal better with the con artist than another con artist. The problem youth who is caught up in the spirit of change and helping others will expect nothing less than total honesty from his peers.

Once such a young person finds a positive means of self-expression he may display much greater enthusiasm in helping others than do those who have always been "well adjusted." The youth who has become positive by choice rather than by upbringing knows not only the pain of living with unsolved problems but also the personal triumph that comes in mastering hardships. This motivation should not be surprising; it is well known that the convert to a movement often displays more zeal than the regular.

[Margin annotation: conversion]

Strong and reforming youth present to those not yet committed to change

*In sociological literature, this concept has been given a rather formidable name, *retroflexive reformation*, which means the individual becomes involved in the reformation of others, thereby changing himself.

Can it
Cause
~~~~~~~
Skeptisism?

a particular challenge whose influence cannot readily be dismissed. The new member in a group knows that this reforming peer has experienced many of the same problems, and his word has to be given special credibility. Criticism cannot be viewed as it would be if it came from an adult or from a "square" peer; criticism is not condemnation or rejection when it comes from a concerned peer. In time, the new member looks to the changing member and says, in effect, "If he could do it, so can I." Such is the strength of the aggressive problem maker who becomes the aggressive problem solver.

NOTES

[1] Saul Pilnick, Albert Elias, and Neale W. Clapp, "The Essexfield Concept: A New Approach to the Social Treatment of Juvenile Delinquents," *Journal of Applied Behavioral Science* 2, No. 1 (1966).

2

Issues in
Positive Peer Culture

> Trust not him with your secrets, who, when left alone
> in your room, turns over your papers.
> —Johann Lavater

TRUST AND OPENNESS VERSUS
INVASION AND EXPOSURE

Some confrontation groups use strong group pressure to break down a person's defenses in order to compel "honesty." A target of such a group is sometimes referred to as "being on the hot seat." Trying to defend against interrogation but subjected to intense attack from the group, he eventually breaks under the strain of prolonged confrontation. Defenses are shattered, a flood of emotion comes forth, and the inner person is bared for the scrutiny of the group. The climate of these confrontation groups is one of *invasion and exposure.*

In contrast, PPC seeks to build a climate characterized by *trust and openness.* The young person in a PPC group does not enter a group to be placed on the hot seat; rather, he is, in effect, in the help seat, and his peers' preoccupation is to show their concern for him. This is no minor distinction.

PPC groups have no concern other than to be of help. Groups are never empowered with the "right" to punish, harass, restrict privileges, exclude, or in any other way hurt a member. PPC is based on the application not of peer *coercion* but of peer *concern.* While peer concern may sometimes lead to peer pressure, PPC has no place for pressure without concern, for such is only psychological intimidation.

9

While many strong feelings may be shown in a PPC group meeting, the goal is not to force an unwilling youth to bare his emotions. Advocates of exposure procedures may define a good meeting as one in which somebody "breaks down." While an individual should feel free to express any feeling to his group, achieving some catharsis in which all comes pouring out is not the object. For this reason, PPC groups usually are less threatening to a young person than are groups based on intense confrontation and exposure.

Table 2.1 compares the PPC approach with the confrontation approach as each might be seen through the eyes of a new group member. The chart shows that PPC assumes initial fear and distrust to be normal responses as one enters a group. The youth who has experienced disillusionment in past human relationships has no reason to believe that he should trust other group members. This distrust is not a "sick defense" but the appropriate response to a world that has not always been safe. The person who enters a group that is intent on exposing him feels very much alone, an outcast. If he resists the advances of a confrontive group, the members become more and more adamant; should his defenses hold, the group becomes frustrated and the attack increases to an almost unbelievable barrage of screaming and shouting that nobody would interpret as "caring."

A recent newspaper account of a group program built on the notion of confrontation and exposure emphasizes this problem:

> During the *first day* at the home, Charles experienced the most *harrowing* one-and-a-half hours of his life. In a *searing confrontation* with fellow delinquents to determine whether Charles was *redeemable* and could be *accepted* into this group. . . (italics added).

It might be asked what gives any group of strangers the right to engage in a searing confrontation with another person. The poet Sir Rabindrinath Tagore wrote: "He only may chastise who loves" [1]. Further, we wonder who has the wisdom to determine whether a person is "redeemable" or not. In PPC group members never sit in judgment with authority to reject one another.

PPC assumes that the young person will initially distrust the group, which bears the burden of proof that distrust is groundless. During the vulnerable initial days in the program, the other members offer assistance to the new youth rather than exploit him. They learn that the newcomer's superficial behavior must be tolerated for a while, for any attempt to destroy his front will frighten him and perhaps drive him away from the group.

Many group programs have been criticized for the way they collapse defenses that have been constructed over a lifetime. This concern is valid. PPC does not assume that people with problems need to be forced into communication; the young person in a PPC group does not enter into some once-in-a-lifetime episode of contrived communication with a group of strangers. Rather, foundations are laid for a lifetime of experience with care, concern, and mutual trust.

Table 2.1. Comparison of PPC versus confrontation approach

Positive Peer Culture: *Missonary Work* Trust and openness *Good Teaching*	Confrontation groups: Invasion and exposure
1. I am afraid of showing myself to the group.	1. I am afraid of showing myself to the group.
2. The group tells me that in time I will feel free with them. They tell me about themselves.	2. The group tells me that I must be totally honest with them. They try to find out about me.
3. I feel safe as the group shows me they will not hurt me or take advantage of me.	3. I feel uneasy because they are trying to make me tell them things I don't wish to divulge.
4. The others are bringing out their problems and seem to feel good about it. Why shouldn't I face my problems, too?	4. The others say I am being phony, but I can't see any reason why I should tell them anything. Why should I face my problems.
5. My defenses do not seem necessary; so I let down my guard.	5. My defenses are not strong enough; so they break down my guard.
6. I open up to the group.	6. I am exposed to the group.
7. I have been strong enough to bring out my problems.	7. They have been strong enough to uncover my problems.
8. I feel better after opening up. I don't believe they would use anything I said against me.	8. I don't know how I feel after being exposed. I am concerned that they might use something I said against me.
9. When a new member joins the group, I will know he is afraid and distrustful.	9. When a new member joins the group, I will know he is a phony and dishonest.
10. I will help him get used to the group just as they did when I was new. If he finds it hard to trust, I will continue to help him so that he does not have to be afraid.	10. I will attack him just as they challenged me when I was new. If he won't be honest, I will continue to apply more pressure until I discover what he is hiding.

> What man actually needs is not a tensionless state, but rather the striving and struggling for some goal worthy of him.
>
> —Victor Frankl

A CLIMATE OF CHANGE VERSUS
A CLIMATE OF SECURITY

Many believe that young people should be reared in a safe, secure environment, free of problems and conflict, but present knowledge of human behavior suggests this is an overly simplified notion. People do not develop strength of personality in the absence of some challenge and frustration. Youth need opportunities to experience difficulties and surmount problems in order to learn how to cope effectively with the vicissitudes of life. PPC does not offer youth a sheltered environment where they are protected from the demands of the real world. Students are not provided with highly nurturant relationships in which they become overly dependent on adults; instead, they must learn to relate to one another in new and adaptive ways.

Staff strive with great energy and commitment to instill in young people a desire to change. Ideally, all staff interventions would be positive and even inspirational in nature, but such situations will seldom suffice to produce change. In addition, a climate in which all hurting or self-destructive behavior is challenged is much more conducive to change than is the settled, "leave everything as it is" tone that dominates many traditional programs. Change occurs most readily when social equilibrium is disrupted. In an overly secure and tranquil environment, many youth are not in the least motivated to change; when all is going well people seldom see any need to alter their behavior. Therefore, if movement is to occur youth may first have to become dissatisfied with things as they are.

Many young people are not even aware of the dangerous or destructive nature of their behavior. Our schools are populated with students who experience very little anxiety about their problems because, having achieved a sort of equilibrium, they have very little desire to alter their behavior or to test their values. A student may be engaged in almost suicidal abuse of drugs and still feel that he has no problem. A youth may steal but be concerned only that he not get caught; that he may be hurting another individual does not seem to bother him. The provision of greater security will not help to change these young people; rather, they must be motivated, perhaps even prodded, to begin the process of change.*

Many youth workers are reluctant to apply pressure to young people or to create stressful situations for them. These adults often treat young people as fragile beings because they do not want to add to their conflicts or to make

*At this point, the reader may be troubled by the apparent contradiction between our previous discussion about creating a climate of trust and the present concept of avoiding a climate of security. No contradiction really exists, but the reader's sense of dissonance is real because the separate concepts of PPC are seldom seen together, usually having been thought to be incompatible. (For example, it is easier to imagine a combination of peer control and adult permissiveness than a combination of peer control and adult authority. It is also easier to fathom a program based on trust and security than one based on trust and change.) Much of the leverage of PPC is in its combination of concepts that are thought to be polar but really are not. Our only advice to the reader is to "stay loose" and avoid trying to stereotype the program. PPC is a total system, and systems can best be understood in learning about the various parts and seeking to avoid reaching premature closure.

them feel guilty. Certainly, a few are so emotionally inadequate that they need a highly protected environment, but they are exceptional cases; the vast majority, even those with many problems, are quite capable of handling challenging or uncertain situations.

Instead of being guilt-ridden and overly anxious, many youth (particularly delinquents) do not experience enough guilt and so may need to become more anxious in order to be motivated to change. They must come to feel uncomfortable and ill at ease each time they hurt themselves or others.* Of course, no one would advocate purposely exposing youth to continuous, excessive anxiety; yet all too often anxiety has been viewed as totally bad (a synonym of emotional disturbance) and its positive aspects overlooked. Anxiety is not undesirable but essential—the body's natural warning system to signal that some change in behavior may be necessary. If a person is driving an automobile toward a curve at an excessive rate of speed, we hope he will experience some anxiety that will motivate him to reduce his speed. Anxiety signals the individual that "all is not well." A person without anxiety would have no warning system, no way of knowing when his behavior was contrary to his best interests.

Adults who work in a PPC program are as likely to create as to alleviate anxiety. When properly managed and directed, anxiety can facilitate the process of change. We do not mean that anxiety is useful at all times, in all situations, and with all students, but when used in a carefully planned manner, significant benefits can accrue. If a student becomes anxious enough about a problem, he will be motivated to take action.

> Many of the boys in a school for delinquent students had stealing problems. Staff locked up everything, even each boy's personal belongings, making theft impossible but leaving the basic stealing problem unsolved. Then one day staff removed all of the locks, causing the students to become very anxious because they had no way of protecting their possessions. Staff used this anxiety to point out that if some in the group had problems with stealing, then the group was responsible for helping these people to solve their problems. Soon stealing, which had been seen as "cool," came to be viewed in quite a different light.

PPC does not promise a young person a world of contentment, security, and freedom from anxiety; rather, a climate is created where all behavior that hurts another person is noticed and challenged. Anxiety is aroused in the young person, and he begins to question his existing values. As the youth is awakened to his lack of concern for self and others, he is already becoming a better human being.

*Psychoanalytic writers also have noted this phenomenon. If the patient is comfortable with unacceptable behavior, the therapist may seek to make "ego syntonic behavior" become "ego alien."

> The path of duty lies in what is near at hand, but men
> seek it in what is remote.
>
> —Japanese Proverb

HERE AND NOW VERSUS THEN AND THERE

PPC focuses on the direct and immediate problems of an individual. PPC groups do not become entangled in an analysis of all the unusual details in a person's history; neither does PPC search for answers to a person's problems by looking "outside" the person to family pathology or community disorganization. PPC groups do not become engaged in theoretical debates of social, philosophical, or political issues. Instead, young people are asked to concentrate on their own behavior and feelings in the current real-life situation.

A widespread misconception holds that one must analyze early childhood experiences in order to understand his present difficulties. The notion is that once a person is able to achieve "insight" into the origin of his behavior, his problems can be readily resolved. However, experience does not always support this idea. After years of psychotherapy, many people become veritable experts on their own dynamics, and yet they continue to be just as unhappy and troubled. It is not sufficient to learn that one's behavior is the result of "early maternal deprivation" or "unresolved Oedipal anxieties." In fact, this kind of interpretation of the origins of one's problems is generally of little value.

Workers who prefer to concentrate on the here and now are sometimes defensive about the accusation that they are not handling truly important matters. Somehow the feeling persists that those who do not dig out material long buried in a person's unconscious must be dealing in trivia. But what is really meant by *depth*? If a worker is not probing deep into case-history dynamics, does this mean he is therefore dealing only in superficialities? The word *depth* is really a biased word. We have heard workers describe themselves as "depth counselors," but who ever heard anyone's claiming to be a "shallow counselor"? The issue is not a simple controversy between depth and superficiality as some would like to make it appear.

People with problems sometimes consume much therapy time talking about remote, trivial, and nearly forgotten events when it would be much better to work on tangible, relevant, present problems. We are not saying that it is never of value for an individual to relate his present problems to past experiences. To the contrary, an important part of the problem-solving process in PPC is the life story an individual communicates to his group, because as the members gain perspective on the person's past they are better able to help in the present. However, the goal in telling one's life story is not to achieve insight but to help the group see how the youth views himself.

Further, the very act of sharing oneself is of great value, for the student is now invested in others: "I have told you about myself; so now I am a part of you."

Sometimes individuals avoid real-life problems by becoming engrossed in philosophical discussions. PPC groups do not become sidetracked in such considerations as "the changing sexual morality" or "the politics of race relations." While such discourse might well have educational value, it gives too easy an opportunity for verbally skillful students to intellectualize instead of dealing with their own immediate problems. Also, PPC does not strive to encompass all of the educational topics often included in traditional counseling programs, such as "selecting a college" or "how to choose a vocation." As important as these concerns may be, they are not the focus of PPC and therefore should be handled in another context.

PPC groups do not occupy time in "psychological" discussions in which sophisticated terminology obscures individual behavior. Further, groups do not engage in acting out situations (psychodrama), in developing "sensitivity" through exercises in communication, in videotape analysis of behavior, or in any other such procedures. Rather, PPC is built solely around the solution of real-life problems. The learning that results from solving actual problems translates much more readily into future behavior than does the learning that results from artificial exercises in communication.

> Trouble is what you make it.
> —Edmund Cooke

PROBLEMS AS OPPORTUNITY VERSUS PROBLEMS AS TROUBLE

PPC sees a problem as a very special opportunity for change rather than as a mishap. Those who view problems as trouble frequently go to great lengths carefully to arrange the environment to avoid the creation of problems, and when they do occur the goal is to halt the deviant behavior as rapidly as possible. However, trying to stamp out problems is often like trying to squeeze the air out of a tied balloon: either the air shifts to a bulge on the other side of the balloon, or the balloon breaks. Many attempts at suppression only force the problem to reappear in another area or cause an explosion.

Perhaps the most telling example of failure in attempts to suppress problems is noted in many traditional correctional schools. Here, delinquent youth are confined in a highly structured environment where behavior is as totally controlled as possible. Sometimes the attempts at control backfire, and youth openly rebel. However, most of the time students present a placid profile, at least when adult control is present. Youth usually learn to serve their time quietly, making a superficially positive adjustment. Then they are released from the institution only to become reinvolved in difficulty within the community. This is the dynamic underlying the startling rates of recidivism (often as high as 75%) common to many correctional schools.

PPC makes a distinction between (solving) problems and (controlling) problems. (Although it works toward the goal of solving broad patterns of problems, PPC also acknowledges the necessity of controlling harmful behavior. The issue of behavior management is discussed more fully in Chapter 9.) Traditionally, schools and youth agencies concentrate on "controlling" problems. The more recent and highly sophisticated behavior-modification programs also are limited to altering specific behaviors without regard to attitudes, values, or feelings. PPC does not consider it sufficient to modify only observable behavior. A person can discontinue a specific troublesome behavior (e.g., stealing) and still maintain negative social values and a poor self-concept. PPC believes that most problems result from distorted social values and/or a distorted self-concept. Only as a person adopts positive social values and develops a positive self-concept can his problems be fully resolved.

Although learning theory is employed in PPC (e.g., positive behavior is reinforced by group approval), the focus of PPC is different from most behavior-modification programs. Controlling undesirable behavior pre-emptively fails to acknowledge its parameters, which usually include a set of values and attitudes. The expression of negative values and behavior is permitted, even encouraged, in PPC, so that youth have the opportunity to make a clear choice. Typically, they are surfaced, examined for their utility, and then rejected in favor of the prosocial norms imbedded in the positive peer culture. This opportunity is not available in more current behavior-management programs. The ability of most operant management systems to influence behavior is quite potent as long as external reinforcers are continued. However, with an adolescent population the continual reinforcers that peers provide are more potent and lasting than behavior managers have thus far been able to introduce.

Table 2.2 compares the PPC concept of problems with that of approaches geared to behavior elimination or control. As this comparison shows, PPC sees problems as normal. The existence of problems should not greatly embarrass anyone. People with problems are in no way viewed as abnormal. The important consideration is that a person be aware of his problems and do something to solve them.

In contrast, the popular viewpoints are that problems reflect mental illness, immorality, emotional disturbance, or ignorance. It is easy to see why many people feel they must go to such lengths to deny problems: to admit having problems is to admit being defective. Thus, individuals seek to hide their problems to escape being labeled as abnormal.

Table 2.2. Comparison of problem solving using PPC and other approaches

Solving problems	Controlling problems
1. Problems are a normal part of every person's life	1. Problems are abnormalities in people (often viewed as mental illness, immorality, ignorance, or deviant behavior).
2. People with problems are no different from all other people: they sometimes hurt themselves or others.	2. People with problems are different, because they show behavior that is objectionable to society.
3. Acknowledging that one has problems is really a sign of strength.	3. Acknowledging that one has problems is really admitting to an abnormality.
4. It is all right for problems to be shown.	4. It is not good to show problems.
5. When problems arise, those around the person have an opportunity to help him understand the problems and to become more considerate of himself and others.	5. When problems arise, those around the person should try to get him to stop showing this troublesome behavior.
6. Problems cease to be a concern when the person no longer needs to hurt himself or others.	6. Problems cease to be a concern when problem behavior can no longer be observed.

If problems are not shown, it is hard to know how to begin solving them. A teacher of remedial reading would find it difficult to improve a child's reading skills if the child never spoke to show just what his reading difficulties were. Only as the teacher can see and analyze the child's reading errors is correction possible. So it is with personal problems. *PPC sees the appearance of a problem as an opportunity; as a person's problem becomes visible, the way to a solution becomes clearer.*

In most settings, teachers and youth workers attempt to suppress problems because they fear a loss of control. This concern is valid particularly when work is with large numbers of students. The potential for contagious troublesome behavior is high in any group of students who does not relate positively to authority. Thus, the adult moves quickly to squelch any acting-out behavior. One of the common interventions is to "kick out" the troublemaker. Students who are viewed as a negative influence on other students are sacrificed for the sake of the rest of the group.

Kicking out problem youth has many negative side effects.

1. Some understudy usually is waiting in readiness to fill the role of chief troublemaker.
2. The attempt to make an example frequently backfires as other students vent hostility toward adults in defense of one of their number.

3. For the youth who already expects to fail, the threat of possible exclusion may lessen motivation to succeed.
4. Sometimes the student who acts out with defiant bravado in reality receives some reinforcement from expulsion.

PPC does not communicate to failure-oriented youth that "we are upset by your problem." Rather the message is: "It is good that you are showing your problems, because now something can be done about them." A strong program will never develop if youth are allowed to fail. Kicking out a youth is really giving up, which can only weaken everybody involved.

1. The troublesome youth has failed to overcome his problems so he is less likely to succeed in the future.
2. The peer group has failed to help one of their members so they will have less confidence in their capacity to handle the problems of other members.
3. The adults have failed to build a group that could succeed and will be more likely to feel unable to handle difficult youth.

Staff must help the group to accept all problems as their responsibility. One does not abandon a person just because he needs help more than most. Instead, group and staff strength must be mobilized to deal with any problem, however difficult. If the problem cannot be resolved, then every student and every adult may have to admit that this one individual has more power than all of them combined.

While PPC staff allows problems to emerge, they do not sit back in a permissive manner as chaos develops. Problems must occur at a tempo at which they can be monitored and examined, not at a landslide rate. As problems emerge, the students' responsibility is to use them in a constructive manner; the adult must see that the group assumes responsibility for resolving them.

NOTES

[1] Radindrinath Tagore, *The Crescent Moon* (New York: Macmillan, 1913), p. 22.

3

Demanding Greatness Instead of Obedience

> Great persons are able to do great kindnesses.
>
> —Miguel de Cervantes

As adults encounter the challenge of difficult youth, the typical response is to demand conformity and obedience. Elaborate sets of rules are concocted and then the search for ways to enforce them begins. Rewards are offered to students for behaving, and punishments are applied to keep them from misbehaving; adults send for reinforcements; students are shunted to special programs—but still the problems persist.

Rather than demand obedience, PPC demands that young people become the mature and productive human beings they can be. Unfortunately, many adults do not really believe that young people possess the quality of "greatness," which is perhaps not surprising since youth seldom are provided with opportunities to display their true human potentials. PPC is concerned with setting expectations high enough to challenge the young person to do all he is capable of doing. To expect less is to deprive him of the opportunity of feeling as positively about himself as possible.

Many teachers and youth workers have long been aware that demanding conformity and obedience was not an effective way of dealing with adolescents, but they usually knew only one alternative: the granting of total freedom. Many attempts to give responsibility to young people are instead really "freedom" approaches. In these programs, adults sometimes totally abdicate authority and return all decision making to the young. Not sur-

19

prisingly, a common outcome is that the students run loose in a manner reminiscent of the classic novel *Lord of the Flies* [4].

Sometimes attempts are made to institute self-government among young people. In most cases, this self-government is in reality a sham. Most public school student governments, in which youth are allowed to decide little more than the color of crepe paper for the school prom, fall into this category. Usually adults do not really want to give up their power; so they make sure that youth do not have much territory to govern.

PPC makes no pretense of turning over all decision making to the students. Adults never abdicate their authority or responsibility. Instead PPC is so designed that adults are in control without controlling. A flight instructor does not give full control to the student pilot but is always available to take charge if hazards are encountered while the student learns to fly. So in PPC, adults assign responsibility to youth and then teach them to follow through on that responsibility.

The notion of heavy demands on students is not altogether fashionable, and traditional mental health concepts have sometimes been interpreted to say that setting high expectations actually is harmful for young people; hence, those with problems sometimes have not been sufficiently challenged to use the strength they possess. These ideas were criticized by Victor Frankl.

> If architects want to strengthen a decrepit arch, they increase the load that is laid upon it for thereby the parts are joined more firmly together. So if the therapists wish to foster the patients' mental health they should not be afraid to increase that load through a reorientation towards the meaning of one's life [3].

This is the demand of greatness in PPC. PPC defines greatness as showing positive, caring values. PPC groups help members to learn helpful and nondelinquent ways of handling themselves and meeting their needs. Youth must come to reject all behavior that in any way hurts self or others and to replace it with behavior that shows care and concern for others.

VALUES OR RULES?

In PPC, youth are not given a complicated road map of explicit rules they must follow. While rules obviously are necessary in any society, still young people must be able to make decisions when no clear rules for behavior exist. Too often rules are geared to keeping unruly youth in submission and meeting the adult's need for control. Adult rules do not prepare a young person to live responsibly amid the complexities and uncertainties of the real world. While our students may learn to obey all the rules we concoct, they may still fail miserably at the business of living. All too often rules give youth an easy way out of having to make wise and independent judgments.

Youth must learn how to make sound decisions even in the absence of specific guidelines.

> A prominent federal judge has a large law library in his office. On an adjacent wall he has placed a sign with the familiar ethic, "Thou shalt love thy neighbor as thyself." Beneath the sign an arrow points in the direction of the thousands of law books, and another inscription notes, "All else is explanation."

Young people must learn the basic values for living and not merely memorize a set of rules.

PPC does not tell youth that they should stop their behavior to avoid punishment, for perhaps they are intelligent enough to avoid being caught. Youth are not told to alter their behavior because it is logical; honesty may not always be logical, and a case sometimes can be made for a crime. Is it always more logical to work at low wages as a domestic servant than to accept employment as a well-paid prostitute? Why should a person work at a tedious job if he has the skills to be a successful thief? PPC does not develop logical arguments against every misbehavior but turns instead to the ultimate issue of values: Is this helping or is this hurting?*

While PPC is oriented toward the teaching of values, we should emphasize that this reference is not to middle-class values or any specific ideology. Rather, there is one basic value—the value of the human being. Such a value is tied neither to social status nor to culture and does not become obsolete with the passage of generations. Anything that hurts any person is considered wrong, and people are assumed to be responsible for caring for one another. Caring means "I want what is best for you." This value is reflected in the thinking of the Judaic–Christian tradition and in most other ethical systems.

MAKING CARING FASHIONABLE

A positive peer culture can exist only in a climate of mutual concern. However, since most youth do not initially show strongly positive, caring behavior, how can caring be made fashionable to them? This question is considered in the remainder of this chapter.

Positive values at the outset often are more acceptable to female than to male groups. The normal societal expectations for women reflect the values of service, caring, and giving of self to others. Thus, the central values of a PPC program are compatible with the role behaviors society has long

---

*The authors are aware that, theoretically, this judgment is not always simple to make. A question is sometimes raised about the conflict between the interests of the individual and the best interests of the group. The ethical dilemma is, of course, the classical, and we will not attempt to reopen the debate here. Fortunately, most problems of young people do not pose such complexities.

advocated for the female. Certainly not all girls manifest kind, helping, sensitive behavior, nor does either sex have a monopoly on hurting behavior. Still, almost all girls have clearly been socialized toward positive caring behavior and thus are not initially likely to challenge the underlying values of the PPC program.

Among male delinquents, the task of making caring palatable is much more difficult. Many young males consider positive, helping behavior as feminine in nature. It is widely assumed that male delinquency is related to the strong preoccupation with manliness that is seen among boys reared in predominantly mother-centered environments. Because of a preponderance of female-based households and the absence or inadequacy of male models, many boys are highly anxious about their sex-role identification and seek to become "real men" as quickly as possible.

The youth gravitates to a male adolescent peer group in search of status and belonging. In the lower-class culture, the measure of manhood is found in the traits of *toughness* (bravery, daring, and other behavior that proves one is not soft or feminine), *smartness* (not intellectualism but ability in conning, verbal putdowns—"playing the dozens"—and hustling), and *autonomy* (resisting control or domination by others) [5]. Observers have noted that the same insecurity about sex role is present in middle-class male youth [6].

The youth strives to imitate the toughness, smartness, and autonomy he observes in his peers. He feels he must always appear strong, and he is very vulnerable to a challenge or dare lest his peers consider him "chicken." Hence, the male delinquent rejects what he feels are feminine values (learned from his mother) in order to prove his masculinity. Cohen has clearly described this process.

> Children of both sexes tend to form early feminine identifications. The boy, however, unlike the girl, comes later under strong social pressure to establish his masculinity, his *difference from* female figures. Because his mother is the object of the feminine identification which he feels is the threat to his status as a male, he tends to react negativistically to those conduct norms which have been associated with mother. . . . Since mother has been the principal agent of indoctrination of "good," respectable behavior, "goodness" comes to symbolize femininity, and engaging in "bad" behavior [proves] his masculinity [1].

Since it is virtually impossible to persuade delinquent males to accept a role they regard as weak and sissified, the group leader must present caring as a strong and masculine activity. The group leader can do this in two ways.

Modeling: A male leader can himself provide a direct model of helpful, positive, caring, and yet masculine behavior. The group leader must show the youth how to redirect the pseudomasculine delinquent toughness into a more appropriate masculine role. The youth needs to learn that the true man is one who is strong enough to stand up for his conviction and be of value to others.

Relabeling: Staff must constantly reverse the valence of helping behavior through a *relabeling process.* Helping behavior is referred to in such terms as strong, mature, and powerful, while all hurting behavior may be referred to as weak, immature, and inadequate. Further, the leader never attacks the youth's desire to be strong but instead redirects this motivation. The youth is not told "you are not so tough as you pretend to be"; rather, the leader embraces and challenges the youth's need to be strong: "Somebody as strong as you will really be able to become a great group member; helping takes strength." In time the youth will cease to view delinquent behavior as cool and come to see positive, helping behavior as desirable and even fashionable.

We have noted that the problem youth frequently has labeled his problem behavior as cool, sophisticated, and fashionable, and sees "good" behavior in a negative light. Whenever this distortion of values is reflected in the language of young people, staff must relabel the behavior so that hurting behavior will be made undesirable and helping behavior fashionable. Thus, for example, if the delinquent youth perceives criminal types as cool, mature, smart, and masculine, then we might counter this view by noting that many 50-year-old criminals are locked in cages because they act like babies and must be watched all the time.

If "truancy" has an exciting quality to it, we ought to give this problem a label that sounds less mature, perhaps "playing games of hide and seek." If delinquent youth feel that their mass rape of a girl is cool, then we should relabel this act as "messing over a helpless person." If stealing is seen as slick, then it should be relabeled as "sneaky and dumb." If a youth gets some rewards from his tendency to act in violent ways, then the attractiveness of such behavior can be diminished when it is relabeled as "having a childish temper tantrum" or "acting like a hothead." If a youth brags about his fighting prowess ("I gave him a knuckle sandwich"), staff can relabel it by asking, "Do you mean you hurt him?" Likewise, if the group under the guise of helping is possibly communicating a veiled threat (e.g., "You had better change or we will be climbing on your back"), staff can question the intent by posing new labels: "Does that mean hurting or helping?"

The general concept is this: Delinquent behavior is often accompanied by a romanticizing terminology that reinforces such behavior. Staff in a PPC program are alert to these terms and attempt to lower the attractiveness of the behavior by calling it by a name that is undesirable to the youth. Likewise, all reference to positive, helping behavior should be made with labels that are desirable. This will produce a state of dissonance* that will

---

*The concept of cognitive dissonance was first developed in Festinger [2]. This theory holds that two cognitions are in a dissonant relationship to each other if they appear to be contradictory; since a state of dissonance is psychologically uncomfortable, the person is motivated to reduce dissonance, perhaps by changing an attitude.

motivate youth to develop negative attitudes about negative behavior and positive attitudes about positive behavior. This is the essence of "making caring fashionable."

PPC staff quickly become adept at describing all positive helping behavior with adjectives associated with strength and maturity and relabeling all hurting behavior with adjectives associated with weakness and immaturity. Many labels are useable. Thus, reference to positive behavior as *great, intelligent, independent, improving, winning* will help to make such behavior more desirable for most students, while the description of negative behavior as *childish, unintelligent, helpless, destructive, copping out, losing* will help to establish such behavior as undesirable and unfashionable.

Certain labels are more effective with boys' groups than with girls' groups, and vice versa. For example, reference to positive behavor as *sensitive, lovely, attractive* may be helpful with girls' groups but may have just the opposite effect with boys' groups. In the same way, the description of positive behavior as *brave, daring,* and *gutsy* will be useful with male groups but will not achieve the same effect with female groups.

It cannot be emphasized too strongly that <u>any negative label is meant to apply to behavior rather than to person; otherwise we are attacking a person's self-concept.</u> Staff and groups should not get into a situation in which they are merely calling a young person names under the pretense of helping him. We can label an individual's explosive behavior as a *childish* temper tantrum, but we should never tell him he is a child; rather, that he is too mature to continue such childish behavior. Since group members pick up many of the relabeling techniques, staff must keep alert in honoring this subtle but important distinction. "Sometimes you act in babyish ways" is quite different from "you are just a big damn baby."

PPC seeks constantly to undercut negative behavior as it continually builds up a person's positive self-concept. The transformation of values that can occur as the positive potential of an individual is challenged is seen in the following account of a 17-year-old youth who was serving his third term in a large, state training school.

Richard: Part 1: Richard had spent almost 3 of his 17 years incarcerated on charges of assault, theft, and truancy. A stockily built, defiant youth, he was a threat to other students and to staff who had to control him. Richard was always ready to fight anyone who crossed him in some way. Because of his hostile behavior he frequently had to be forcibly removed from the cottage or classroom and placed in lockup for several days at a time.

Richard married shortly before his third commitment, and his wife was soon to deliver a baby; so he was particularly eager to earn an early release. Nevertheless, one day he again had to be placed in the lockup cell because of his behavior. Out of frustration and disappointment that he would lose his upcoming release, Richard turned his hostility inward. He tied together pieces of clothing to make a rope, put it around his neck, fastened the other end to a pipe on the ceiling of his cell, and tried to hang himself. A youth in a neighboring cell heard what was happening and summoned the security officer, who cut down the makeshift rope and revived Richard.

This account is an extreme instance of a program that seeks to produce obedient and conforming behavior. Frequently, the effect is only to engender further resistance in the acting-out youth. Richard happened to be in an institution that was in the process of converting from a custodial confinement program to PPC. Although he was not in the PPC program yet, the staff consultant with the new program used the opportunity provided by his attempted suicide to apply the concept of *demanding greatness rather than obedience.*

The usual institutional response to such a suicidal attempt would have been to transfer the youth to the state institution for the mentally ill. However, in Richard's case this procedure was not followed. Staff were sure that Richard's suicidal act did not derive from some episode of psychotic depression or other mental illness; rather, they saw in Richard a great deal of strength, which usually came out in rebellious behavior, in an unwillingness to be controlled by others and a strong desire for independence. Instead of removing demands from Richard and attempting to lower his anxiety, staff placed a different type of demand on him. Assuming that he had positive potential to be helpful to others, they demanded that he use this potential. The account of the PPC consultant's contact with Richard indicates the kinds of demands that are placed on young people in a PPC program.

> *Richard: Part 2:* The consultant told Richard the following. "You are sitting in here feeling sorry for yourself. Here you tell us you have a wife and she is going to have a baby. How are you able to be man enough to produce a child but not man enough to be a real father to this little child? You are feeling sorry for yourself, but who is feeling sorry for that little kid you are going to have? He is not even born yet and he almost didn't have a father. When he gets a little older, what do you think he will say when other kids ask, 'What does your Dad do?' Is he going to tell them that his Dad died in a boys' training school, that he acted like a big baby who could not face the world and so one day went and hung himself?
>
> "Richard, you have no right to mess over another human being like that. What gives you the right to take away your little kid's father? Your child deserves to have a *man* for a father. How are you ever going to learn to become a man, sitting helplessly in this cell and feeling sorry for yourself? This afternoon we are moving you out of this cell and putting you in the cottage for the youngest boys as a helper."
>
> "In the little kids' cottage you are going to get plenty of practice being a man because the boys there really act like a bunch of babies. They scream and fight and sass the staff and have to have someone older watching them all the time to keep them out of trouble. They really are difficult to handle, and you are going in there to get another chance to be a man instead of a child. You are going to be allowed to help the staff with those little kids, and when you show that you have learned how to be a man and take care of little kids, then we will know you are ready to get out of the training school and go home to help your wife take care of your own child, to be that great man he needs for a father."

Richard was transferred from lockup to the junior cottage. About three weeks later one of us had the opportunity to meet Richard for the first time. As we entered the cottage Richard stepped forward, standing about a foot taller than all of the others there. "Hi, I'm Richard," he said, proudly introducing himself. "I am helping work with the fellows in this cottage. I tell you, these little kids here sure need to grow up. I used to be just like them. I was always getting into trouble and then feeling sorry for myself. But not anymore. I am married you know, and my wife is going to have a baby any day now. So I am getting practice working with these boys, and when I get good enough at it, I am going to go home and help with the baby. This group here (gesturing to the younger boys gathered around him) sometimes act just like a bunch of damn babies. That one there is acting today like the biggest baby in the cottage. Now this fella here, he's coming along fine, and we're really going to make a man out of him. . . ."

Several weeks later, Richard was released from the training school to return to his wife and newborn son. Instead of attempting to demand conformity and obedience from Richard, the adults demanded that Richard become the great person that he potentially could become. Richard responded and grew toward responsibility as a husband and father.

NOTES

[1] Albert K. Cohen, *Delinquent Boys: The Culture of the Gang* (Glencoe, Ill.: The Free Press, 1955), p. 164.
[2] Leon Festinger, *A Theory of Cognitive Dissonance* (Evanston, Ill.: Ross Peterson, 1957).
[3] Victor Frankl, *Man's Search for Meaning* (Boston: Beacon Press, 1963), p. 107.
[4] William Golding, *Lord of the Flies* (New York: Putnam, 1959).
[5] Walter B. Miller, "Lower Class Culture as a Generating Milieu of Gang Delinquency," *Journal of Social Issues* 14, no. 3 (1958).
[6] Talcott Parsons, "Age and Sex in the Social Structure of the United States," *American Sociological Review* 7 (1942).

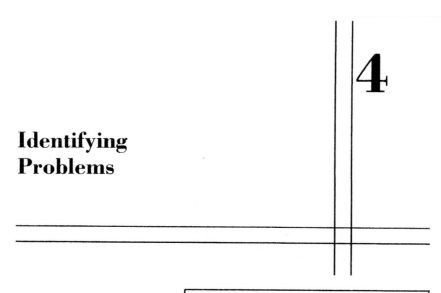

Identifying
Problems

> They do certainly give very strange and newfangled names to diseases.
>
> —Plato

Humans have been identifying and labeling the problems of other humans for at least as long as recorded history. From the days when problems were thought to arise from evil spirits or demons to the invention of today's complex psychiatric terminology, men have tried to create systems for classifying problems in the hope that such systems might somehow lead to solutions.

Classifications are now so complicated that it is not possible for behavioral scientists to communicate with one another about the nature of problems. A room full of social scientists has as many definitions of "schizophrenia" or "psychopath" or "character disorder" as the number of persons in the room. No review of the psychological literature will clarify what the names for problems really mean; one current revision of a standard psychiatric dictionary proudly states that the volume contains over 4000 new terms not included in the prior edition. This number is not a testimonial to the progress made in studying people's problems; rather, it is an admission of the confusion and chaos that pervade the field of "problemology."

In any setting where adults work with youth, we may encounter many different professions, each with a separate language. The teacher, psychologist, psychiatrist, social worker, recreation worker, childcare worker, judge, and parent all are on different wave lengths; everybody views the problems of youth differently and does not understand the language of anybody else.

Amid all this babel we have often judged most valid the professional language that describes problems in the fanciest terms. Most people now know what *paranoid* or *neurotic* or *compulsive* mean, since such psychiatric terms are in common use. The layman has come to stand in awe of psychological terminology and strives to acquire the terms as his own, if only to be able to carry on seemingly enlightened social conversation.

THE VERNACULAR OF PROBLEMS

PPC uses as little "profession" jargon as possible. In place of "psychologese," a set standard, straightforward *universal language of problems* has been developed for use by all youth and adults who are part of a PPC program. All discussion of problems revolves around an easily understood set of labels covering most of the difficulties young people may experience. These terms include three general labels and nine more specific labels.*

1.	Low self-image	
2.	Inconsiderate of others	General problems
3.	Inconsiderate of self	
4.	Authority problem	
5.	Misleads others	
6.	Easily misled	
7.	Aggravates others	
8.	Easily angered	Specific problems
9.	Stealing	
10.	Alcohol or drug problem	
11.	Lying	
12.	Fronting	

Since a problem is defined as anything that damages oneself or another person, all problems theoretically can be encompassed within "inconsiderate of self" or "inconsiderate of others." If a behavior or feeling does not in any way hurt another person or the self, it is not a problem. Although "low self-image" overlaps with "inconsiderate of self," the first is so pervasive that it merits a special place on the list. Since a classification system with only two or three categories would not facilitate clear and precise communication, several additional specific problems are included. These labels refer to particular patterns of troublesome behavior that occur quite frequently among youth.

The discerning reader already might have noted many connections between the first three general problems and the subsequent nine specific problems. For example, a student who is easily misled may really have a

*The format of a "vocabulary of problems" develops from the Guided Group Interaction tradition.

very low self-image. Before one can resolve the basic problem, though, it may be necessary to focus on more specific problems. A group may readily notice that a youth is always led into trouble by others, but it may initially fail to recognize the more subtle connection with self-concept.

The group learns to identify the problems a young person displays, to help one another understand them and to help in their resolution. Simply to eliminate the expression of negative behavior is not the goal; the youth who truly resolves his problems will possess new positive and quite valuable social skills.

POSITIVE PEER CULTURE
PROBLEM-SOLVING LIST

The Problem-Solving List (Table 4.1) defines the characteristics of the young person who has resolved the problems. Students and staff in PPC programs receive this statement of goals, and individual progress is measured against the specific targets set by the list.

Although the idea of a universal language is not new, the implementation of such a vernacular in an educational or treatment setting is uncommon. The effect of having all students and staff share a common language is a dramatic improvement in ability to communicate. The staff will not need a separate set of terms; in fact, formal progress reporting also can be done with this terminology by attaching a copy of the Problem-Solving List to the report for clarity. For example, in settings where youth are referred to PPC by juvenile courts, the regular communication of progress to the court is in the form of a monthly letter written in the vernacular of the Problem-Solving List. This report is made available to group members and staff and is sent to the agency that assigned the youth to the program.

Experience suggests that it is not useful to add other problems to the list. Any longer list becomes cumbersome and difficult to learn and causes much quibbling in categorizing the behaviors. Likewise, changing the labels of the problems on the list may cause unanticipated difficulties. Several examples may suggest the reasons for apparent omissions from the vocabulary of the list.

Observers frequently ask why *fighting* is not listed as a problem. The word *fighting* evokes too many contradictory images to be viewed as a problem. Because of the positive aspects of fighting for what is right (for one's country, against crime, and for survival), the term is ineffective as a problem designation. The negative behavior itself is better described as "aggravating others" or being "easily angered" or "inconsiderate of others," none of which carries the positive connotations of fighting.

Another question may be why *sex problems* are not specifically included on the list. Because students must accept the list as a valid description of problems, the inclusion of such a sensitive subject would be threatening

Table 4.1. Positive Peer Culture Problem-Solving List

Problem	When solved
1. *Low self-image*: has a poor opinion of self; often feels put down or of little worth	Is self-confident and cannot easily be made to feel small or inferior. Is able to solve his problems and make positive contributions to others. Doesn't feel sorry for self even though he may have shortcomings. Believes he is good enough to be accepted by anybody.
2. *Inconsiderate of others*: does things that are damaging to others	Shows concern for others even if he does not like them or know them well. Tries to help people with problems rather than hurt them or put them down.
3. *Inconsiderate of self*: does things that are damaging to self	Shows concern for self, tries to correct mistakes and improve self. Understands limitations and is willing to discuss problems. Doesn't hurt or put down self.
4. *Authority problem*: does not want to be managed by anyone.	Shows ability to get along with those in authority. Is able to accept advice and direction from others. Does not try to take advantage of authority figures even if they can be manipulated.
5. *Misleads others*: draws others into negative behavior	Shows responsibility for the effect of his behavior on others who follow him. Does not lead others into negative behavior. Shows concern and helps rather than taking advantage of others.
6. *Easily misled*: is drawn into negative behavior by others	Seeks out friends who care enough about him not to hurt him. Doesn't blindly follow others to buy friendship. Is strong enough to stand up for himself and make his own decisions. Doesn't let anyone misuse him.

7. *Aggravates others*: treats people in negative, hostile ways

Gets along well with others. Does not need to get attention by irritating or annoying others. Gets no enjoyment from hurting or harrassing people. Respects others enough not to embarrass, provoke, or bully them.

8. *Easily angered*: is often irritated or provoked or has tantrums

Is not easily frustrated. Knows how to control and channel anger, not letting it control him. Understands the putdown process and has no need to respond to challenges. Can tolerate criticism or even negative behavior from others.

9. *Stealing*: takes things that belong to others

Sees stealing as hurting another person. Has no need to be sneaky or to prove himself by stealing. Knows appropriate ways of getting things he wants. Would not stoop to stealing even if he could get away with it.

10. *Alcohol or drug problem*: misuses substances that could hurt self

Feels good about self and wouldn't hurt self. Does not need to be high to have friends or enjoy life. Can face his problems without a crutch. Shows concern for others who are hurting themselves by abusing alcohol or drugs.

11. *Lying*: cannot be trusted to tell truth

Is concerned that others trust him. Has strength to face mistakes and failures without trying to cover up. Does not need to lie or twist the truth to impress others. Tells it like it is.

12. *Fronting*: puts on an act rather than be real

Is comfortable with people and does not have to keep trying to prove himself. Has no need to act superior, con people, or play the showoff role. Is not afraid of showing his true feelings to others.

Table 4.2. Description of problem

Problem	Description
1. *Low self-image*: has a poor opinion of self; often feels put down or of little worth	**a.** Feels unlucky, a loser, rejected, mistreated; feels sorry for himself; has no confidence he can be of value to others. **b.** Worries that something is wrong with him, feels inadequate, thinks he is good for nothing, is afraid others will find out "how bad I really am." **c.** Distrusts others, feels they are against him and want to hurt him, feels he must defend self from others. **d.** Is uncomfortable when people look at him or speak to him, can't face up to people confidently and look them in the eyes. **e.** Is insecure with "superior" people, doesn't feel good enough to be accepted by others except those who also feel poorly about themselves.
2. *Inconsiderate of others*: does things that are damaging to others	**a.** Does things that hurt people, enjoys putting people down. **b.** Acts selfishly, doesn't care about the needs or feelings of others. **c.** Seeks to build self up by manipulating others for his own purposes. **d.** Takes advantage of weaker persons and those with problems. **e.** Won't help other people except, possibly, if they are members of his own family or circle of friends.
3. *Inconsiderate of self*: does things that are damaging to self	**a.** Puts self down, brings anger and ridicule on self, does things that hurt self. **b.** Acts as though he doesn't want to improve self or solve problems. **c.** Tries to explain away his problems or blames them on somebody else. **d.** Denies problems, hides from problems, runs away from problems. **e.** Doesn't want others to point out his problems or talk about them but resists help with problems.
4. *Authority problem*: does not want to be managed by anyone	**a.** Views authority as an enemy camp "out to get him." **b.** Resents anybody's telling him what to do, does not readily accept advice from either adults or peers. **c.** Can't get along with those in authority, gets into big confrontations with authority figures, often over minor matters. **d.** Does not respond well to parental control or supervision.

32

e. Tries to outmaneuver authority figures, circumventing or manipulating them if possible.

5. Misleads others: draws others into negative behavior
a. Seeks status by being a negative or delinquent leader.
b. Gives support to the negative or delinquent actions of others.
c. Misuses others to achieve his own goals, getting them to do his "dirty work."
d. Wants others to be in trouble with him, afraid of being separate.
e. If others follow him and get in trouble, feels that it is their problem and not his responsibility.

6. Easily misled: is drawn into negative behavior by others
a. Can't make his own decisions and is easily controlled by stronger persons.
b. Can't stand up for what he believes, even when he knows he is right.
c. Is easily talked into committing delinquent acts in order to please or impress others.
d. Behavior varies from good to bad, according to influence from those with whom he associates.
e. Lets people misuse him, is willing to be somebody else's flunky.

7. Aggravates others: treats people in negative, hostile ways
a. Make fun of others, tries to embarrass them and make them feel low.
b. Seeks attention in negative ways, irritates or annoys people.
c. Makes subtle threats in word or manner.
d. Challenges, provokes, or hassles others.
e. Intimidates, bullies, pushes people around.

8. Easily angered: is often irritated or provoked or has tantrums
a. Frequently becomes upset or explosive but may try to excuse such behavior as naturally "having a bad temper."
b. Easily frustrated, unable to accept failure or disappointments.
c. Responds to the slightest challenge or provocation, thus making other people's problems his own.
d. So sensitive about himself that he cannot stand criticism or disagreement with his ideas.
e. Easily upset if someone shouts at him, points a finger at him, touches him, or shows any negative feelings toward him.

9. Stealing: takes things that belong to others
a. Thinks it is all right to steal if you are sneaky enough not to get caught.

Continued

9 priority problems

Table 4.2 (Continued)

Problem	Description
10. *Alcohol or drug problem*: misuses substances that could hurt self	**b.** Doesn't respect others and is willing to hurt another person to get what he wants. **c.** Steals to prove he is big and important or to prove he is "slick" enough to get away with it. **d.** Steals because he is afraid peers will think he is weak or chicken if he doesn't. **e.** Doesn't have confidence that he could get things by his own effort. **a.** Afraid he won't have friends if he doesn't join with them in drugs or drinking. **b.** Thinks drugs are cool, tries to impress others with his drug knowledge or experience. **c.** Uses the fact that many adults abuse drugs (such as alcohol) as an excuse for his involvement. **d.** Can't really be happy without being high, can't face his problems without a crutch. **e.** Acts as though he doesn't care about damaging or destroying self.
11. *Lying*: cannot be trusted to tell truth	**a.** Tells stories because he thinks others will like him better. **b.** Likes to live in a make-believe, fantasy world. **c.** Is afraid of having his mistakes discovered and so lies to cover up. May even make up false problems to hide real ones. **d.** Has told so many lies that he may lie even when there is no apparent need to lie. **e.** Twists the truth to create a false impression but doesn't see this as lying.
12. *Fronting*: puts on an act rather than be real	**a.** Needs to appear big in the eyes of others, always needs to try to prove himself. **b.** Bluffs and cons people, thinks loudness and slick talk are better than reason. **c.** Acts superior, always has to be right, argues, needs to be best in everything, resents being beaten. **d.** Clowns or shows off to get attention. **e.** Plays a role to keep from having to show his real feelings to others.

enough to prevent young people from entering willingly into a program that appeared to focus on such issues. We do not mean that sexual problems are not discussed in PPC groups; rather, they may be discussed as they relate to a person's self-image or as to being inconsiderate of self or others.

Family problems are discussed in PPC but are not given the status of a place on the problem list; the presence of "family problems" on the list would allow a young person to flee to safety behind the handy excuse of a troubled family rather than directly face his own problems. *Withholding information* is not a problem in PPC because it would encourage the group to attack rather than build trust with the distrustful member who cannot communicate readily. Nor are *manipulating, playing around,* and *not showing feelings* given status as formal problems since they do not necessarily cause harm to self and others.

Contemporary slang words for problems should not be substituted on the problem list, although the peer group may not necessarily be discouraged from using such expressions in their discussions. Most slang expressions have emotional connotations that interfere with the proper and serious consideration of a problem. For example, the slang term *ripoff* has a much more daring, flippant, and masculine image than does the somewhat more "sneaky" concept portrayed by the word *steal*. The problem labels on the list are neither supportive nor highly disparaging. Rather, the tone is mildly negative to neutral, which allows the youth to communicate about problems in an objective manner and makes the list equally useful to all individuals, adult and youth alike.

Problems can be identified and labeled with relative ease and consistency because of the straightforward nature of the list. However, since the list encompasses a wide range of behavioral problems, the staff in a PPC program should clearly understand the precise meaning of the various labels in order to prevent any distortions in communication that may result from the different meanings that different individuals attach to the labels. In the remainder of this chapter, we list the 12 basic problems (Table 4.2) and provide more identifying information about each. Again, the descriptions are written at a level to facilitate ready communication of the concepts to all students and staff involved in the program.

While the foregoing is a Pandora's box of negative behavior, it is essential that *problem solving* not be seen as a negative process. In an insightful discussion of "the problem with problems" Panzino [1] cautions against overwhelming youth (who already doubt their own abilities) with excessive crirticism in the guise of assigning problems. The focus must not be on every trivial flaw in a person but on self-defeating patterns of problem behavior that can be surmounted. Furthermore, embodied in most problems is some latent strength: An authority problem may signal courage or assertiveness; stealing and lying may reflect cleverness and quick thinking. One who misleads others is in fact a leader, and one who is misled may be trusting and cooperative. The perfectionist may be easily angered, and the persistent person may be aggravating to others. Finally, fronting, substance abuse, and low self-image are often negative expressions of the need to belong and be accepted which is universal in the human experience.

NOTES

[1] Anthony Panzino, "The Problem with Problems." Paper presented at the Ninth Annual Conference, National Association of Peer Group Agencies, Columbus, Ohio, October 13, 1983.

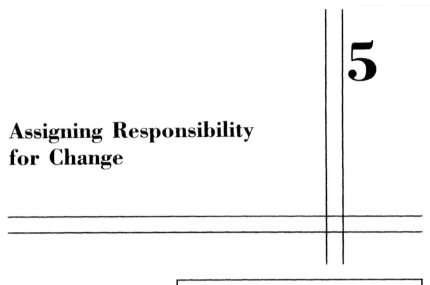

Assigning Responsibility
for Change

> We have forty million reasons for failure but not a single excuse.
>
> —Rudyard Kipling

THE DISPLACEMENT OF RESPONSIBILITY:
"PUTTING IT OFF"

Troubled youth inevitably develop elaborate systems for displacing responsibility for their problems onto some other person or circumstance. When we ask a youth why he got into trouble he will say his parents were messed up, or he had the wrong friends, or the police were out to get him, or the teachers hated him, or his luck turned bad. Projecting, denying, rationalizing, and avoiding, he becomes expert at escaping responsibility. But only as a person feels accountable for his actions is he able to learn from his experiences and resolve his problems.

All of us discover early in life that we can avoid self-examination by looking outside ourselves. If the problem can be attributed to something external to the self, we need not go through the sometimes painful process of change. Adults often unwittingly reinforce young people's tendency to project blame on others. We ask a youth what is the matter with him and then listen patiently to an account of what is the matter with others.

Certainly most of the problems among young people are somewhat related to inadequacies in the family or the community. In fact, many adults encourage youth to conceptualize their problems as parent-related, perhaps hoping to spare them the guilt feelings about problems not of their own creation. It is not at all uncommon for a sophisticated youth to enter

37

willingly into long "therapeutic" discussions about the intricacies of mother's neurosis or father's character disorder and the dynamics of parental conflict but run quickly for cover if the focus is transferred from the parents to his own problems. However, the existence of problems in other family members should not be allowed to excuse a person from working to improve himself.

When it seems impossible to effect dramatic change in the family, workers may develop an attitude of futility; the problems are thought to be inexorably attached to "the family situation." Many who deal with youth have fallen into this trap again and again. In fact, some counseling services will not even work with a young person unless the rest of the family also enters into treatment. Although youth and their parents certainly should attempt to resolve their difficulties, we cannot base the future of every young person on the hope that his family will be rehabilitated.

If the family actually has no strength, then it is much more important that the young person develop the strength to face his own problems instead of seeking someone to hold his hand as he wails at his parents' weakness. After all, the young person will soon become the next parent, and the chain of difficulties that links one generation to the next must somehow be interrupted.

Problem youth also are very effective at shifting the blame for their troubles to the helping adult. Most persons who work with youth will go to great lengths to convince the young people that they are fair adults. Some at times almost beg youth to trust them. When they say, "Look, I am an open and honest person, and if I make mistakes with you, I will admit it," the young people oblige by providing an almost continual report on the adult's errors, inadequacies, and hypocrisies. When the youth says, "You are being unfair," the worker often plunges into a discussion of how to be more helpful but seldom helps the youth to see how he might have evoked these difficulties.

If students assume responsibility for resolving staff problems, then they will have little time for their own. Adults must rigorously police adult performance so that the young will be free to concentrate on the problems of their own making.

In PPC, the demand for responsibility is absolute. All attempts to shift the blame for problems away from self will be countered by peer group members or staff. As one excuse is found to be implausible, a person usually creates another. Again, this new excuse must be seen for what it is: an attempt to put off onto others a problem that belongs to oneself. Since a youth might have spent years trying to convince others (and himself) that the blame lies elsewhere, he usually finds it difficult to honestly face himself. He must come to realize that in pointing out his problems, the helping adult is not attacking him or trying to make him dislike himself. In time, the young person will come to understand, as Aldous Huxley once noted, that the only corner of the universe you can be certain of improving is your own self.

> Responsibility is the first step in responsibility.
> —W. E. Dubois

THE REVERSAL OF RESPONSIBILITY:
"TURNING IT BACK"

Since young people have a well-developed system for displacing responsibility for problems away from themselves, staff must develop an equally effective system for shifting the responsibility back where it belongs. *Reversing* is the process of placing responsibility for action back on those who must do the changing rather than allowing them to project it outside themselves. An almost endless number of reversal techniques can be used; all have in common the fact that they serve to put the student in such a bind that he cannot escape the responsibility for dealing with his own behavior. For example:

> *Student:* I got in trouble because both of my parents are alcoholics and don't care about me.
> *Staff:* Do you mean that all people with parents who have problems get in trouble?

Here staff assumed that the youth was trying to use his parents' problems as justification for his own behavior; so they employed a reversal response, which had the effect of making the youth fully responsible for his behavior and unable to call on the excuse of troubled parents.

When a girl in a residential program ran away, staff asked the other group members why they didn't do something to detain her. The interaction and reversal of responsibility:

> *Student:* We didn't know she was going to run away.
> *Staff:* Oh, you mean she was smarter than all the group?
> *Student:* Well, no, we thought she might run away but we didn't know for sure.
> *Staff:* You thought she was going to run away but did nothing.
> *Student:* Well, is it our job to watch her every minute? We had other things to do.
> *Staff:* There was something more important than helping her not to hurt herself?

Another youth left a residential treatment center and when he returned used the excuse that he went to see his girlfriend.

> *Student:* I went to see my girl, I hadn't seen her for two months.
> *Staff:* Didn't she want to see you?
> *Student* (puzzled): Yes, that is why I went to see her.

Staff: She doesn't want to see you at home full time, then? Just once in a while when you go truant?

Student: No, she would like to have me all the time.

Staff: Then why do you do things that keep you here and at the same time say you want to go home? Don't you care enough about her to solve your problems and get home to her full time?

A youth had been working on a serious drinking problem, but when his brother came home on furlough from the army he went on a weekend drunk and was arrested. In explaining away his behavior, he tried to put the responsibility on his older brother, and staff countered with a reversal.

Student: Well, I really quit drinking but only did it this week because my brother wanted to.

Staff: Do we understand that you are saying you don't have a drinking problem but now you have a new problem of being easily misled by others?

Many problem youth justify their negative behavior by the provocations of others. This process is "responding to putdowns" and is exemplified by the following interaction.

Student: I hit him only after he called me a name.

Staff: Names bother you?

Student: Yeah, that bothered me. Do you like to be called names?

Staff: We are talking about you. Did you do something to get him to call you a name?

Student: I didn't do a thing to him.

Staff: What do you think that shows, when someone goes around calling people names for no reason at all?

Student: There must be something wrong with him.

Staff: How do you mean?

Student: He has a problem. . . . Oh, I see, I should have helped him with his problem instead of making it my problem, is that what you are saying?

Frank became angry when confronted by his group, had a temper tantrum, hit the wall with his fist, and broke his hand. When he returned from the hospital 2 days later, he had a cast on his hand and attempted to blame the group for provoking him, thereby causing him to hurt himself. The group and staff refused to accept this projection, instead pointing out that his own problem had brought on the trouble, and he would have to learn to deal with his problems. Seeing that his strategy was not working, Frank changed his approach. He tried to get the group's sympathy by saying that the doctor had said he might not have all of the movement in his hand, that it was his right hand, that he was planning to go into an occupation that required use of his hands, and now because of his injury he might not be able to use one hand, not be able to get the kind of job he wanted, and so on. One of the group members reversed this situation by telling Frank: "My 10-year-old brother has crutches and wears braces up to his chest, but he doesn't complain and feel sorry for himself as much as you do." Since Frank obviously did not like the comparison, he immediately abandoned his strategy and became more appropriate in his interactions.

Another variation of reversing responsibility is seen in this example.

> *Student:* It is my life, I can do with it what I want.
> *Staff:* Is Ann saying she has a right to mess over herself and to hurt those who care about her?

Or one student who refuses to help another justifies his position by saying he doesn't like the other.

> *Student:* I ain't going to help him, I can't stand him.
> *Staff:* If you were walking down by the river today and you saw a little kid fall in, would you pull him out?
> *Student:* Heck, yeah, I would pull him out.
> *Staff:* Even if you didn't know him or like him?
> *Student:* Of course, I would still pull him out.
> *Staff:* Well, I guess you do understand about helping people even if you don't like them.

When a new person in the group does not seem to be working on his problems and the older members are not doing enough to help, it may at times be helpful to say to the older members, "Do you think you are ready to leave the group when this new student hasn't even started to work on his problem? We may be able to tell how ready you are by how well you get the new student going on working on his problems." Or the interaction may go like this.

> *Staff:* What are you doing to help him?
> *Student:* We are just taking our time.
> *Staff:* Well, perhaps time is something you have plenty of. Staff will probably be working here for years; so whenever the group decides to care then people with problems will have a chance.

On rare occasions, one encounters a new youth who totally resists entrance into the group, even to the point of adamantly refusing to attend meetings. Instead of becoming locked in combat with such a youth, the staff may find reversing responsibility to be more effective.

> *Student:* You are not going to get me to attend that group meeting.
> *Staff:* Fine, you need not go to the group now; you may not be ready. It takes strength to be able to help others. It also gives us a chance to see how you are changing, to find out when you are ready to go home . . . when you are willing to help others. You can let the group members know when you care enough about them to help them.

Problem youth frequently try to set up incidents in which the adult is placed in a helpless, defensive position. Whenever possible, staff should reverse these situations so that the student and not the adult bears responsibility for the problem.

> A teacher was giving a sophisticated 14-year-old delinquent youth an individual achievement test on one of his first days in a new school. He began in a disinterested manner and soon told the teacher he was not going to take the test and wanted to go back to the classroom. The teacher coaxed, humored, and even pleaded with the youth to take the test, but in the midst of the appeal the student got up and walked out of the testing room, leaving the teacher to talk to herself. It would have been better if the teacher had reversed the problem to the student, perhaps by saying, "You are not ready to take this test yet," and then discontinue the testing.

Many groups of young people try very hard to figure out the staff because they are looking for ways to manipulate the adult rather than to change themselves. Sometimes staff are lured into discussions in which students ask them to reveal facts about their private lives. While on the surface this activity may appear innocent (in fact, the staff member may even assume he is developing an open and warm relationship with the students), the situation is potentially hazardous, for students often use such information against the staff in a later attempt to predict, control, or manipulate. Staff need not put much effort into attempts at discriminating between innocent questions and those that embody some trap. Often it is better to use a reversal to avoid such interactions and shift the focus back to the youth.

> *Student:* Mrs. Peterson, do you drink?
> *Staff:* What does that have to do with your working on your problems?
> *Student:* Oh, I just was interested in knowing whether or not you drink.
> *Staff:* Oh, I see, but I still don't see how this is connected with what you are supposed to be working out.
> *Student:* Never mind.

In using such techniques, staff must be careful not to cut down the student, for possibly he had an appropriate reason for asking. Likewise, we are not suggesting that staff behave in cold and aloof ways, only that they care enough about young people to avoid wasting important time on unimportant issues.

Students sometimes play up to authority figures by giving false compliments designed to ingratiate the adult so that he can be manipulated. For example, the principal of the school meets three or four boys in the hallway. One smiles and says, "Here is The Man." Instead of basking in this assumed compliment, the principal might better reverse the comment by saying something like, "*You* are the *Men,* you have important work to do." Such a response, *if genuine,* can reinforce the young person's sense of responsibility, will not be interpreted as a putdown, and will beg the question of whether or not the young person was sincere in his compliment to authority.

Frequently, youth will raise complaints against staff. Adults should always be alert to possible truths embodied in the criticisms, but it is seldom useful to reinforce them. The group may grumble that they cannot learn anything because of their teacher's stupidity. The principal makes a mental note to check with the teacher whether a problem may exist, but he responds to the group with the comment, "Do you mean that nine cool guys like you can't work with one schoolteacher to make a good class?"

Students are often skillful in using verbal putdowns with one another and with staff. Becoming upset by negative verbalizations and responding to them directly is not so effective as employing a reversal. As this example shows, staff can often reverse the responsibility for problem behavior back to the group as well as to the individual.

> *Student:* You people are all a bunch of retards.
> *Staff:* Does the group understand why Rita thinks she has to hassle others?

An adolescent boy frequently mixed humor with hostility by joking with a particular teacher about his bald head. In the past, the staff had tried a number of approaches, including humor and ignoring the situation, but to no avail. The problem was effectively dealt with by using a reversal procedure.

> *Student:* Did you polish your head again today?
> *Staff:* Do you know, it will really be great when you feel good enough about yourself, John, that you don't have to go around trying to cut other people down.

In PPC staff view everything that youth say and do (or fail to do) as potential material for reversal; such is the magnitude of importance that they assume responsibility for their behavior. This concern communicates to the young people in a continuous process that:

1. We know you have the potential to change.
2. We believe so fully in your potential that we will permit no instances of hurting behavior to go unnoticed.
3. We will reflect your words and actions back to you in a manner such that you can learn to assume full responsibility for helping yourself and your peers.

As one bright, perceptive delinquent was overheard saying after a few weeks in a PPC program: "They even talk to you different. It's like talking into a mirror, and then you find the answer to everything somewhere inside yourself."

Staff will make the greatest use of reversal procedures in the initial stages of establishing a positive culture. Later, these procedures will not be so necessary since the students themselves will become effective in reversing responsibility back to the individual, but the reversal process will set a tone that pervades the entire atmosphere of a PPC program.

Much of the effectiveness of reversals will depend on the attitude, tone of voice, and goal and intent of the speaker. Verbal contests that have a winner and a loser must not develop. Whether the incident is minor or major, the objective of a proper reversal is always the same: to show our care and concern. Unwilling to be diverted, we persist in expecting the best that is within these young people.

Student: I bought the book on Positive Peer Culture and studied it; so now I know what you staff are trying to do.

Staff: Fine; now you will really be able to help.

6

Implementing a
Positive Peer Culture

THE DEVELOPMENT OF GROUP CULTURES

Positive peer cultures are developed in two basic ways: *seeding* and *creating*. In seeding, one transfers students from an ongoing group program into a newly created group. Here, youth with group experience help other youth learn how to operate effective groups. If the proper persons are selected, seeding new groups can be a very rapid and efficient way to start groups, but the students selected must be strong enough to fill this teaching role in a helpful way without putting down peers who do not yet know how to participate in a positive group process.

The second and perhaps most common approach is to *create* a positive culture. Here, staff have the responsibility for transforming the peer subculture, which may be particularly challenging since not all staff in the program may fully understand PPC, and some may not be supportive. Students expect that adults know what they are doing, but if staff are still struggling with and learning about the program, they cannot be so helpful as would be desirable. Thus, considerable responsibility in the early stages falls on the group leader.

If the group leader does not initially have the support of other staff, the administration must support the program. One cannot simultaneously fight against students who resist the program, staff who suspect the program, and

45

administrators who undercut the program. At a minimum, one should have the endorsement either of frontline staff or of administration; then it usually will be possible to concentrate on developing the students themselves, for they will provide the only proof convincing to skeptics. In a sense, it can be said that PPC is started at the student level and then built upward rather than started at the administrative level and then filtered downward.

In some other group programs, it is believed that the group should be left on its own to develop its culture. Experience has shown that this method generally disenchants staff and group members alike, because such a laissez-faire approach requires the group to go through a long, frustrating ordeal before it reaches optimum peformance. Furthermore, since PPC groups are open-ended, with membership continually changing, the initial group culture could continue for years, being transmitted to many successive generations of members. It is important to establish a culture that will adequately serve all students who may pass through the group.

Stages of Group Development

In new groups, four generally recognizable stages mark the group progress from origin to the point of effective functioning.

1. *Casing.* In the first stage, students and staff are not comfortable with one another, since no discernible group structure exists. At this point, students usually attempt to seek information about one another and the staff but avoid showing themselves. During this highly defensive stage, they may seek out a scapegoat in a weak member or in the adult staff.

2. *Limit testing.* As the students begin to reveal their basic personalities and true behavior, they gravitate into cliques. Individual members begin to experiment with techniques of participating in group meetings (perhaps even to mouthing the right words), but their ties to previous negative values continue, and thus considerable negativism can be expected. A great deal of tension is generated around revealing oneself and one's feelings about other members. Although students start to recognize their own distinctive problems, they cannot yet function as a truly positive group.

3. *Polarization of values.* As the students discover alternatives to their previous values and behavior, they are brought to the point where they must decide whether they really want to change. Cliques and subgroups become more tenuous and crumble away, producing much anxiety. At this stage, hostility may be prevalent within the group or directed toward the leader by factions of the group. Gradually, a common sense of purpose develops among some of the group members. Those who have started to adopt a new value system now are bound with a strong sense of mutual solidarity and a beginning group identification. Those who are unable or unwilling to accept new nondelinquent roles may react antagonistically, struggling to regain negative influence; when they fail, they may withdraw, even to the point of running away.

4. *A positive peer culture.* This is the final stage, when the students have formed a strong, cohesive, clique-free group that embodies a value system of mutual care and concern. The group relies less and less on adult leadership and places considerable demands on its members to face their problems, to help one another, and to work eagerly on the problems of the more defensive new students in the group. At this stage, the old members become virtual social workers on a 24-hour basis. These youth are nearing readiness to return to the broader culture.

The Group Leader's Role in Culture Building

A positive peer culture is achieved only as a group is brought successfully through these several stages of development. Each stage has its own particular challenges and requires specific patterns of response from staff. Let us consider the role of the group leader in these stages.

Casing. In the first meeting, the leader begins with an explanation of why the group program is being started, perhaps indicating that the youth must have some intelligence, strength, and leadership potential, which is why these particular young persons were selected. The leader does not indicate that he alone is there to help but, rather, tries to tune the group members in to one another. He gives sanction to caring and presents it in a manner acceptable to the students' life-styles and outlooks. At this stage, the group leader keeps in low profile, encouraging all interactions, positive or negative. In a nonauthoritarian, nonjudgmental fashion, he supports almost any form of verbalization, conveying approval and acknowledging group members' comments and suggestions.

The group leader may subtly allay some concern about the group by pointing out the confidential nature of the discussions. He may establish credibility for the program by indicating that it is not some new and untried experiment, but that many other young people have been able to develop successful PPC groups. The leader may also comment on the groups he has started or observed, since early establishment of his credibility as a leader of groups is helpful. It is sometimes useful for the new group to visit a strong, positive, existing group, to view videotapes of other groups, or to listen to a tape recording of an established group.

The leader then becomes involved in teaching the format and procedures of the meeting. He avoids playing traditional roles, which may worry the members, since they would be more secure if they knew just what to expect from him. Although he is fairly active in discussion, he does not answer questions authoritatively or respond to attack. Neither does he go out of his way to make the group members comfortable; it is not his job to fill in every silence with commentary to "get it going" or to "figure it out." While he strives to present himself as a warm, concerned adult, he does not try to make the group dependent on him but continually refers group members back to one another for answers.

The leader communicates a confidence in the students' competence to do what has to be done to build a group. He conveys the attitude that "You are good people and I am sure you will be able to do it." In the initial meetings, he establishes the group rules on confidentiality, expectations of caring, and the procedures of pointing out problems. He informs the members of their responsibility to recommend one another for release from the group as problems are solved. He is alert to ways to inspire the youth toward helping one another and tries to convey his total commitment in believing in the great potential of his group.

If the leader encounters resistance, he does not reinforce negative members who may be seeking to assert status by upsetting him. He stresses the positive without trying to apply negative sanctions to antagonistic expressions. He does not confront or argue, and he never tries to give a tough guy or superior impression but communicates, instead, a relaxed, confident, interested attitude. He never implies that the difficulties youth encounter are the staff's fault, nor does he try to defend himself or other staff. Rather, he makes the problem belong to the students.

Outside the meeting, the group leader is totally involved with the group yet maintains a social distance, refusing to become involved in ordinary social tête-à-têtes. He refers all questions to the group. He begins to confront individual students on their behavior, initially, perhaps, on minor issues so as to focus problems without engendering hostility.

Limit testing. At this stage, the leader should expect several weeks of testing. The group will cover the terrain rather well, trying to find a way to get out of the program or divert it to some end other than helping. They may blame staff, say they want to quit the group because nothing is being accomplished, claim not to care about other members, come late to meetings, or sit in silence. The group leader need not counter or win all these encounters; rather, he calmly reverses the problems and displays his continuing confidence that the group will come to see the wisdom of helping, and they are smart enough and strong enough to care.

The group leader encourages candid expressions, whether positive or negative. He may even subtly reward youth who have the courage to express dissatisfaction with the program. While at this stage, he may ignore verbal hostility, but any physical violence immediately evokes his strong response.

The group leader at this stage is more or less biding his time, as the group learns the structure of the program and becomes dissatisfied with venting only negativism in their new-found freedom of expressing unconventional attitudes. The group may begin to put on a superficial front of positive activity. The leader works with this front, knowing that in time positivism can become genuine. He does not confront the members on their superficiality, for when the members begin to trust one another they will no longer need fronts.

The group leader begins to challenge the group to assume responsibility for all behavior of its members, refusing to exercise control functions. He begins to teach members to analyze the group process and become sensitive to the harmful nature of members' behavior.

Outside the meeting, he becomes more critical of the group members' behavior. He begins to make the members feel uncomfortable and employs the coordinated assistance of other staff who are dealing with the students. He still avoids standard social conversation and maintains his social distance. While some members now may be seeking him out individually, he avoids such individual conferences unless the contents are fed back to the group. The leader thereby neutralizes manipulation and avoids being tied to youth who are quick to cling to the adult.

Polarization of values. At this stage, the group leader becomes more selective in the type of verbal interaction he encourages. Since participation is now established, the leader must help the group to learn to discriminate between helpful and nonhelpful communication. He stimulates members to become more aware and concerned about their own and others' behavior. The group is beginning to develop into an effective helping unit.

The group leader escalates the attack on negative behavior by attaching negative labels to it. He begins the movement to isolate negative leaders, if possible without putting down such individuals in front of their peers. Even if the adult has group support, he avoids openly attacking a negative student and, rather, seeks for opportunities to reinstate the youth in leadership roles with positive involvement. (The redirection of negative youth is discussed in considerable detail in Chapter 9.)

Outside the meeting, the group leader reinforces positive, helping behavior. He aggressively points out the seriousness of behavior, but now instead of confronting individuals he turns it over to group members, giving them increasing responsibility and placing high demands on them to deal with problems in a helpful manner. The group is starting to function when its members frown on negative behavior.

A positive peer culture. At this final stage, the group leader helps the group to refine problem-solving skills. He points out the dynamics in the group and helps the members understand their implications. He continues to sensitize the group to instances of hurting behavior that they may overlook. He points out positive changes in members and helps them to maintain a high morale as the group finds pride in their emerging ability to deal with difficult problems. His role in group meetings is less obvious, though he never appears disinterested but continues to model strong concern.

Outside the group, he must now be able to back away from a strong central role and allow it to function with greater independence. He continues to be involved and abreast of what is happening and never assumes that a group once positive will always remain so. He is seldom drawn into individual confrontations but seeks, instead, to draw the group into all problems he may observe. He does very little direct teaching or training and now avoids the instructor role by prompting the students to recall what they have already learned.

He relaxes in his social interactions, communicates more freely, and reveals more of himself as a person than he did in the earlier stages of group development. He continues to maintain his role as a staff member, since it is always conceivable that he may again need to reassert himself should changes in the group climate or constitution cause a regression to some previous level.

THE COMPOSITION OF GROUPS

Several variables should be considered in constituting the membership of PPC groups. If the grouping is carefully done, less difficulty will be experienced in developing and maintaining a positive group culture. Let us discuss here guidelines for group formation.

Effectiveness of Peer Approaches at Different Age Levels

Considerable thought has been given to the question of which age range responds best to PPC. Some have argued that the level of verbal interchange in group discussion makes PPC treatment appropriate only for the older adolescent. It is widely known that advocates of some types of verbal therapy do not claim effectiveness for youngsters below 10 years of age.

However, the most important variable in determining the effectiveness of the peer culture approach is not verbal fluency but the young person's primary responsiveness to influence by his peer group. For the very young child, peer influence usually is secondary to adult influence; for the older youth (15 years of age and above), peer influence generally is of overriding concern; and in the intervening ages (10–14), responsiveness varies considerably among children. Therefore, one might conclude that the more peer-oriented a youth is, the more appropriate will be a peer approach, while the more adult-oriented a child is, the more effective adult-oriented approaches will be.

A peer-oriented approach probably will be more effective at the junior high school level than at the elementary level and probably most effective at the senior high level. Nevertheless, the degree of effectiveness does not preclude the possibility that one could develop programs with a peer influence component at the elementary school level. The central focus of PPC, concern for others, is relevant to persons of any age.

Grouping by Sex

As indicated earlier, PPC groups are composed of youth of the same sex. While counseling has established that one may operate effective coeducational "talk therapy" groups, such groups are not effective in PPC for several reasons.

Research has noted that much delinquent behavior is peer-group related and is prevalent among males who operate in small groups or gangs. The subculture of male delinquents is a social phenomenon unlike the social patterns formed in heterosexual groupings. Some evidence indicates that this sexual pattern of acting-out behavior is changing as females now are involved in a higher pecentage of delinquencies than in the past. While many current youth problems (particularly drug use) may occur in sexually integrated social situations, the traditional single-sex, male delinquent peer group is still central to most delinquency. Until this pattern changes, a peer-culture program will be obliged to work within the existing structure of adolescent peer systems.

A basic assumption in PPC is that youth are primarily responsive to their peer reference group. In the development of a self-concept and self-identity, the adolescent orients heavily toward the reference group of peers of the same sex.* Thus, the male tends to compare himself with other males in evaluating his personality, physical prowess, social competence—in general, his basic masculine self-identity. In similar fashion, the female uses female peers as a reference for her basic feminine self-identity. Even though adolescents are heavily involved in trying to contact and impress members of the opposite sex, their primary standards of reference for self-evaluation are members of the same sex.

Coeducational groups present additional barriers to relaxed, open communication when contrasted with single-sex groups. Because of youth's need to engage in courtship behavior, coeducational groups among adolescents often are characterized by masked communication. Members of both sexes become unduly involved in attempts to impress the opposite sex. Intense two-person relationships that emerge within the group are disruptive to the sense of group cohesiveness necessary for the development of a totally positive culture. Despite increasing sexual sophistication, members of both sexes in coeducational groups exhibit greater inhibitions in revealing concerns about sexual adequacy than they do in single-sex groups. While it certainly could be argued that these inhibitions might offer good material for group discussion, this would be a further complication to a process that is already sufficiently complex.

In residential settings, PPC groups function as units 100% of the time, living, studying, and playing together. For obvious practical reasons, this togetherness also precludes coeducational groups but, of course, does not limit the possibility of regular coeducational contacts within the residential treatment setting.

---

*For a theoretical analysis of reference group theory as it applies to delinquency, see Clark [1].

Group Size

Experience with groups of differing sizes has led to the general guideline that the ideal size of a PPC group is nine members. Why is nine the optimum number and not a smaller group, say of five or six members? When the group is that small, the members are too few to keep the process alive, interesting, and challenging. Input is limited, fewer perceptions and viewpoints are possible, and the adult role tends to be more prominent. The group all too easily evolves into a cozy, self-satisfied "family" without the motivation or capacity to confront its members' problems. Because of the shortage of members, each one is too exposed in group meetings; hence, the group either probes too frequently and intensively or the meetings become boring, tedious, and enveloped in irrelevancies.

When the group is too large, however, another set of problems arises. Individuals do not become the focus of group help often enough, and they are not sufficiently scrutinized by the group. Some students do not have sufficient opportunity to participate in group activities, and the passive youth is almost totally lost in the large group. Communications in meetings easily become garbled because of the number of participants. As the size of the group increases, one loses the feeling of intimacy that is found in the smaller group. A large membership lengthens the process of reporting problems, and the group will have little time to thoroughly discuss problems. Perhaps the greatest difficulty in the large group is that a cohesive, caring group culture cannot develop because of the number of human relationships that must be maintained.

It may be useful to analyze the number of different two-person relationships that exist in groups of different sizes. Figure 6.1 illustrates the added complexity of interpersonal relationships as group membership increases. Table 6.1 shows how the number of two-person relationships increases as each additional member joins the group.

Table 6.1. Group size

Number of group members	Number of two-person relationships
6	15
7	21
8	28
9	36
10	45
11	55
12	66
15	105
20	190

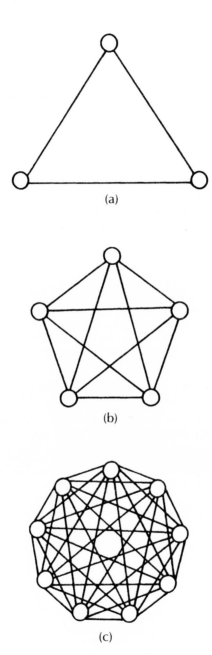

(a)

(b)

(c)

Figure 6.1. Complexity of interpersonal relationships develops as group membership increases. (a) Three-person group has three relationships; (b) five-person group has 10 relationships; (c) nine-member group has 36 relationships.

As the group enlarges it becomes almost impossible to keep track of all the relationships within it. A group of 9 has 36, 2-person relationships, but a group of 20 has 190! This number makes it impractical to run a cohesive and consistently positive group; inevitably, the large group splinters into sub-groups or develops an elaborate status hierarchy.*

Guidelines in Grouping

The goal in grouping is to place each student in a group that will help him to resolve his problems. In general, the best groups are homogeneous with respect to age, sex, maturity, and sophistication. When possible, youth who reside in the same community or neighborhood should be grouped together, since they will be more knowledgeable about one another and will be in a position to carry the influence from the group into the community.

On the other hand, groups function best when they are somewhat heterogeneous in personality and problem type. Thus, a group composed entirely of weak, passive, withdrawn youth will not perform so well as a group with some diversification of personalities. Groups composed exclusively of weak and easily misled youth, or of withdrawn youth, or of youth with the same problem (e.g., homosexuality) generally should be avoided. A group should be racially balanced, although, when possible, the placement of only one or two individuals of a particular race in a group should be avoided.

Groups may contain youth of various physical sizes, but no one should be placed in a group where he can so intimidate others that they are afraid to confront him even with their collective strength. Thus, a large, physically aggressive, delinquent youth should be placed in a group with several others who are near his capacity in physical prowess. The smaller youth can be absorbed in an established positive group where all of the members are larger than he is, but in starting new groups (if youth are highly negative) it is best to avoid placing a small student in a group of larger peers.

A group may have members that span 2 or 3 years. As important as age is the factor of maturity. It is not helpful to group naive, immature youth with those who are mature and sophisticated, because the immature youth will not function with confidence. While many PPC programs use commonsense evaluations of maturity and judgments based on available information about the specific behavior problems of the youth, specific measures of maturity, such as those Warren[†] developed, can be helpful. If a person is much more

*This point is well illustrated by the account of a large cottage group of 20 youths studied by Howard Polsky [2].

†M. Q. Warren's system of classification is described in Warren [4]. For a discussion of the 1-level approach applied to a group-treatment program, refer to Turner, Palmer, Neto, and Warren [3].

mature and sophisticated than the rest of the group, the others will be unable to deal with him.

Another important consideration in grouping is the strength of the staff members. If no staff member has the courage to confront a particular group member, the group probably will not be able to deal effectively with such a student either. Therefore, the strong, difficult youth should be placed in a group where both students and staff are strong enough to avoid being maneuvered or overpowered.

PPC programs have been used with students quite low in intelligence (IQ in the 70s), but since verbal facility is useful in PPC low intelligence can be a handicap. Nevertheless, caring can be practiced at some level by a wide range of students, including those of limited intelligence. In evaluating intelligence, it is important to look beyond the IQ score, for many youth who do poorly on verbal tests are highly verbal in the natural setting.* A reasonable spread of intelligence is fine, but persons who are extremely low in social intelligence and verbal fluency should generally not be placed in a group of highly intelligent, verbal youth, or their limitations may cause further feelings of inadequacy.

Placement of brothers or sisters in the same group is not recommended; experience suggests that siblings usually gain more from the program if they are allowed to operate independently of each other. If both are in the same group, a question of confidentiality sometimes arises, as one sibling is likely to report to the family on the other's communication in the group.

Forming Groups in a Residential Setting

In forming new groups in a residential setting, one must consider the length of time various youth have already been in the program. Recently enrolled students may be readily involved in newly formed groups, but youth who have been in residence for a number of months under another program may present some resistance. Long-term students often are highly motivated toward going home and may view the implementation of the new program as disruptive of that goal; they may feel that the game plan has been changed on them midway through their placement and all previous invest-ment has been wasted. Nevertheless, it is not always possible to start new groups with only new students; it may be necessary to endure this problem until natural turnover provides a fresh population of students.

In any setting where several groups will be in operation, the creation of one group composed primarily of more sophisticated and aggressive youth is a wise idea that existing staff may not receive well when a program is

*Many street-oriented, lower-class youth with limited academic skills are very proficient in the verbal-confrontation game known as "playing the dozens" or "signifying." When redirected, such verbal fluency can be highly useful in the group situation.

beginning; the previous strategy might have been based on the notion of divide and conquer. However, incorporation of the negative leaders into one group can have positive effects. At first, the group really will be a gang rather than a group, and sufficient staff support must be available to deal with the initial problems that will result. Within a relatively short period of time, perhaps 3–4 months, such a group usually can be converted into a positive force. This group then will be able to receive into membership any new strongly negative youth and will not be intimidated by him. If, instead, one spreads the negative students across several groups, the probability will be that they will "take over" other groups. Staff will then have to spread their efforts across several groups in an attempt to counter the influence of the negative students.

When strong negative youth become involved, the program gains credibility in the eyes of other youth in the setting. A group developed only from selected "nice" students would be all but ignored in the social system of the school or institution.

Forming Groups in a School Setting

Several special factors should be considered in starting a PPC program within a community school setting. Teachers may initially assume that the groups are designed for "bad kids" and may want to involve only problem students. While one could build groups with such youth, this situation would alleviate only individual problems while the overall student culture would remain unchanged. Strong positive students also must be included in order to influence the total school subculture. Therefore, many school-based PPC programs have sought to include strong indigenous peer leaders rather than only problem students. These leadership groups are constituted as a voluntary, accredited high school leadership course in order to give a positive connotation and avoid penalizing youth for their participation. Groups should be formed at the outset of a semester or marking period to facilitate proper scheduling of meetings.

Since only a small proportion of the student body can be included in the initial groups, the goal is to select those with the most influence in the various peer factions. The first step in selection is to complete a power structure study. A definition of leadership is circulated to the teachers, and they are asked to identify both positive and negative student leaders, thereby providing the initial pool of names for prospective group members.

All students who have been nominated because of their leadership potential, then, are individually interviewed by the group leader. The purposes and potentials of PPC are explained, and the students are told that the groups are meant for those who really care about people and have enough strength to become involved. They are also asked to suggest persons whom they view as leaders, since they may identify students not included on the teachers' lists.

The group leader himself will spend time in the school, looking for potential leaders not identified by teachers or students. Patterns of seating, associations in the hall, and other informal contacts may point to background manipulators who were previously overlooked.

Using all of this information, two initial groups (nine boys and nine girls) may be formed, drawing from all segments of the school population. The group should include positive and negative students, gifted and slow students, delinquent and drug-oriented students, and students of different racial backgrounds. Other issues related to forming PPC groups in schools are discussed more fully in Chapter 11.

Contraindications for Grouping

PPC groups have included youth with a wide range of social and emotional problems. Some youth are not well suited to this program, however. The youngster who is extremely withdrawn and nonverbal may not function so well as the more verbal and aggressive youth. Likewise, youth who are seriously retarded cannot follow the group's verbal activities. Youth with extremely disorganized personalities (autistics, schizophrenics) may not benefit from placement in PPC groups. Certain highly specific, abnormal behaviors (e.g., anorexia, such neurotic compulsions as fire setting, encopresis, enuresis, tics, and behavior resulting from organic deficiencies) are not ordinarily the province of PPC approaches. However, many of these individuals have broader social problems and poor self-concepts and thus may receive benefit from participation in a peer-group program, even though treatment is not directed at the primary behavioral abnormality. A strong group often is able to provide a positive climate for many types of youth, since they will be treated in humane and helpful ways regardless of their problems.

Changes in Group Membership

Many PPC groups are open-ended, which means that older members leave the group and newer members enter in a continual process. As individual students achieve maximum benefit in resolving their problems, they will be released (by the group members with staff concurrence), and a new member will take the place left open. The rate of turnover in a given group depends on several factors, including the length of stay in a particular program. In residential settings with delinquent groups, the length of stay can be as short as 4 months when the culture is very strong and youth are highly motivated to work on their problems. When groups contain more emotionally disturbed youth, those with limited intelligence, younger delinquents, and youth with weaker personalities, the length of time in the group may be longer. While staff create among students the expectation that working on problems is not necessarily a long process, students must likewise be aware that they will continue in the group until they have resolved their problems. Avoidance of excessive turnover of members at any one point in time is important. If several older members simultaneously leave and are replaced by new members, the culture of the group can be seriously disrupted. Group cohesiveness will diminish and morale will sag with excessive instability of membership.

The decisions on group assignment should be made by staff that have the greatest understanding about the youth's background and the broadest knowledge about the constitution of the groups. Therefore, in a program with several groups, assignment usually will not be decided by staff directly involved with individual groups, since their perspective is limited. In residential settings, some member of the administrative or clinical staff usually is responsible for making placements after reviewing all available information about the individual students and the various groups. If group leaders or other frontline staff are assigned the responsibility for grouping, much competition and conflict can arise.

Group members do not have the power to prevent a new member from entering. PPC is not some sort of closed club in which older members rule on the admissibility of a youth. The group never sits in judgment over a potential applicant by saying, "We will give you another chance." (Second chances are the province of judges who place people on probation; the new member is in no way on probation.) Rather, the group must communicate the spirit that "We will help you no matter who you are." Ultimately, groups can become positive about receiving a member. Even in settings for de-linquent youth the culture can be so developed that when the group is told, "The schools, parents, and courts have given up on this person; what about your group?", the response is, "We'll take him! We can help him!"

One way of replacing a departing student is to "find the original's double." If the group culture is strong and the group membership is well constituted, then replacement of a departing member with someone of the same type of personality is desirable. For example, if a strong, formerly negative leader is leaving, he should be replaced with another individual who shows that behavior. If, however, the group is poorly constituted, a member's departure provides an opportunity to shift the balance of member-ship in another direction.

A new member entering the program is not oriented by staff. Staff members should meet him briefly, welcome him, and indicate an interest in him by asking him where he is from, what grade he is in, and such neutral questions. The group leader will want to indicate subtly to the youth that he "knows about" his situation, but beyond this information, the youth should be referred to the group for orientation. Staff should avoid the temptation to answer the questions that are raised (knowing full well this contact would be a good way to begin building a strong personal relationship with the student), and should tell the youth that the group will be happy to help him get oriented. Total responsibility then is placed on the group.

A frequent question concerns the amount of information the group should have about a new student. In general, the group should receive little or no information, except who the person is and that he "needs help." Distribution of a fact sheet on the background of the new member is not a good idea, for such information disadvantages him in that they all will know about him but he does not yet know them. Moreover, the group leader should not read the new member's record to the group; there is no need to make it "easy" for the group to learn to understand the individual. The group is not entitled to this information so long as trust has not been established, and once the new person trusts the group, members still will not need to see his record because they will have learned to know him better than those who wrote the reports in his file.

New students will be more receptive to positive values expressed by peers rather than imposed by adult authority. Since PPC will be different from any experience the youth has encountered, it is crucial that the members work hard to help him feel part of the group. The first 2 weeks are critical, and the group should be carefully attuned to him during this time. During this initial period the old members will, outside of group meetings, tell the new member about themselves. Since the new member has "missed out" on the life stories of the established members, they are responsible for briefing him. This knowledge will allow him to begin to help all others in the group without being told, "You don't understand; we talked about that before you came here."

If a new student does not seem to be properly placed, the staff tends to respond by asking that the youth be transferred to another group or even removed from the program. Since we should never have placed a youth in a group if we didn't think that group would be able to help him with his problems, any such mistake cannot be blamed on the youth or the group but only on the staff. Transferring the student to another group only communicates to the student and the group that they have been failures, and while problems may be temporarily diminished, the effect of such "failures" on the students is hardly worth the gain, if any. While in extreme situations group transfers may be indicated, usually such procedures are very unwise and fail to achieve the intended aim.

It occasionally happens that a youth who has been released from a program does not succeed and is returned to the group. The general guideline is to return the youth to his original group if some of the original peers or staff are still involved. Sometimes the returning student is not positive about his return; he may be hostile and attempt to blame staff or the program for his failure. Staff and group members must not become defensive about his attitude nor punish him for his failure but should get about the business of putting things back together. The attitude is, "O.K., something went wrong the first time; let's see what happened and fix things so this person can succeed." If the group member feels he has to "start all over again," staff may point out that his prior experience in the group will help him to be that much more valuable to others. If the student tells others he conned his way out of the program the last time, then responsibility for this problem should be reversed to the student, since deceiving others does not solve his problems. In general, staff should help the failing student by directing him away from the failures of the past toward the challenges of the present and the future.

NOTES

[1] Robert E. Clark, *Reference Group Theory and Delinquency* (New York: Behavioral Publications, 1972).
[2] Howard Polsky, *Cottage Six* (New York: Russell Sage, 1962).
[3] J. K. Turner, T. B. Palmer, V. V. Neto, and M. Q. Warren, *Community Treatment Project Progress Report: The San Francisco Experiment,* Research Report no. 8, California Youth Authority (Sacramento, Calif., 1967).
[4] M. Q. Warren, "Classification of Offenders as an Aid to Efficient Management and Effective Treatment," *Journal of Criminal Law, Criminology and Police Science* 62, no. 2 (1971).

Staff Roles
and Responsibilities

7

> Example is always more efficacious than precept.
> —Samuel Johnson

Since PPC is built on the basic values of caring for and helping one another, staff members should be fully committed to the caring process. If adults are not interested in young people but are concerned only with overpowering and subduing them, a positive culture will be much more difficult to establish. Unfortunately, many adults have come to believe that to show concern for students is to weaken adult authority. PPC does not call for soft, maudlin caring. Rather, staff are asked to invest themselves fully in helping youth to develop their potential. Often caring will be shown best when staff place strong positive expectations upon youth. This kind of caring enhances rather than weakens the influence of the adult.

The implementation of any new program often causes staff members to question their roles. They are being asked to risk the instability of change without assurance that the new program will be an improvement. The enthusiasm that advocates of PPC show may only cause further feelings of uncertainty among staff who have had considerable prior experience with "experts" trying to sell the benefits of some program.

Unlike many other programs, PPC has evolved primarily from practice rather than from theory; hence the basic principles, if properly understood, usually are well received by frontline staff. If staff being exposed to PPC can visit an existing program, their firsthand contact with others who have experienced the difficulties of establishing PPC, as well as direct communication with students in the program, will do more to allay their concern than will weeks of arguments, discussions, and staff training.

A DIVERSITY OF STAFF

Staff need not change their personalities in order to be successful in PPC. Too often, we have heard statements about the qualities of the ideal teacher or the ideal parent; unfortunately, we know of none. PPC recognizes that and then capitalizes on the natural differences in staff personalities. Youth insulated in a sterile environment that contains only superbly therapeutic adults will not be properly prepared for the challenges of the real world. Although we certainly do not endorse negative, hostile, or uncaring staff members, a heterogeneity of personalities is nevertheless desirable to allow the youth to confront the problems he will encounter in his broader life experience. The three most important personality types for a PPC program are the *demander*, the *soother*, and the *stimulator*.

The *demander* is the adult most comfortable in an authoritarian role. Usually he sets clear expectations, is willing to confront youth if they fail to meet these expectations, and is viewed by young people as firm, strong, and not easily manipulated. He often accepts the challenge of dealing with difficult students whom other staff cannot easily govern. Many students are not able to deal appropriately with those in positions of authority; the presence of a demander will highlight such problems and will give these youth an opportunity to learn to relate to controlling adults. A person who can relate only to polite, gentle, and friendly authority figures will encounter many problems in a world where these qualities are in short supply. Certainly youth should not enslave themselves to autocratic, tyrannical persons, but they must learn to deal with demanding individuals in a positive rather than self-destructive manner.

The *soother* is skillful at building interpersonal relationships and in communicating a warm, relaxed tone to students. No group should be in a constant state of tension, and the soother can help youth to find those quiet times they need for rest and renewal. In residential settings, the soother is useful on the evening shift as the activities of the day are ending. The soother often is less than comfortable with the authoritative aspects of his role. Some youth never show problems when confronted by a strong demander but become very manipulative in the presence of a less rigid authority figure. The difficulties that arise in these relationships can be used as further issues in working on authority problems.

The *stimulator* is usually adept at motivating students toward creative and productive activity. He serves as a catalyst in the program as he transfers his skills and enthusiasm to young people. The stimulator makes a major contribution toward building the cohesiveness and *esprit de corps* necessary for optimum group performance.

A COMMONALITY OF PURPOSE

Because of the complexity and contradictions that pervade the social sciences, the professional in youth work has been exposed to scores of different theories and philosophies. Unlike his counterpart in the physical sciences, the "people-professional" seldom operates from a clear, systematic model. Instead, he collects, almost randomly, a set of ideas, techniques, and life experiences to formulate his own—sometimes very useful—approach. Unfortunately, success hinges too heavily on worker personality, and few individuals can communicate their approach to others. As a result, a large number of workers use divergent methods in pursuit of conflicting goals.

In contrast, staff in PPC programs should operate with a singleness of purpose and approach. Individual workers are not given free rein to "do their own thing." Rather, PPC staff function within a structured system, filling roles based on specific assumptions and methods. On the following pages are drawings that illustrate the basic roles of staff in PPC and highlight several improper and potentially hazardous staff roles (see Figs. 7.1–7.4).

CREATING A CLIMATE FOR CHANGE

Probably staff's most difficult role is in encouraging the expression of problems while setting sufficient limits so that ultimate chaos does not occur. The attitude is "we want you to show your problems, but of course we do not want to be overwhelmed by them." The expression of problems must continually be presented as good in a sense, and students must know that they will not be hurt or punished just because they have problems; hurt may result if they do nothing about resolving their problems.

Staff do not sit passively on the sidelines, hoping that someday the group will become responsible. Building a positive culture requires both supportive and confrontive roles. Not that one should act the part of a "good guy" one day and "bad guy" the next; staff will work consistently to support the positive potential of individuals in the group and to confront the negative behavior. More confrontation of behavior will be necessary when the group is not positive, but in a well-functioning group the members will handle problems and will need little staff confrontation. The reader should not be confused by our use of the term *confrontation* in this discussion. This does not imply combat but rather a quality of persistence and assertiveness about matters that are crucial for the well being of the young person.

The purpose of any confrontation is to focus attention on problems. Staff

Figure 7.1 Proper staff roles. (a) *Motivating:* staff inspires young people to build a concerned group; (b) *reversing responsibility:* the task of problem solving is turned back to the group and youth are taught to assume responsibility for one another; (c) *guiding:* the group is allowed to resolve problems but staff continues to provide redirection as needed.

(a) Nursing

(b) Overcontrolling

(c) Assuming the group's responsibility

Figure 7.2. Improper staff roles. (a) *Nursing:* sometimes staff are so preoccupied with nurturing and gratifying that youth are kept in dependent, helpless roles; (b) *overcontrolling:* while domineering staff may instill obedience, the real issue is what happens when external controls are removed; (c) *assuming the group's responsibility:* as long as staff are willing to handle all problems, the group will not become strong and effective.

(a) Becoming one of them

(b) Avoiding the group

(c) Losing the initiative

Figure 7.3. Hazards to new staff. (a) *Becoming one of them*: the novice may overidentify with youth hoping to win acceptance; instead, he loses his adult role; (b) *avoiding the group*: the new staff sometimes looks for ways to escape from relationships that make them uncomfortable; (c) *losing the initiative*: new staff often spends most of the energy putting out fires; who is responding to whom?

(a) Overconfidence

(b) Underinvolvement

(c) Employing hybrid approaches

Figure 7.4. Hazards to veteran staff. (a) *Overconfidence:* bolstered by success, the veteran may become cocky and careless; the more invincible he feels the more vulnerable he is; (b) *underinvolvement:* after initial challenges are met, the veteran may become disinterested or mechanical and may assume the group can run itself; (c) *employing hybrid approaches:* once the novelty of the program is gone, staff may try to add their own "inventions;" changes can be hazardous if they do not fit into the total system.

should select confrontations carefully so they do not become entangled in losing battles. It does no good to engage in a power struggle that will end only in a shouting match. If confrontation engenders only hostility and aggressive behavior, nothing will have been accomplished.

In order to counter the manipulative skills of certain youth, staff will need to avoid getting into predictable patterns of behavior that will make it easy for such youth to control them.

> As the new group was being formed two members ran away from the group home. Staff spent much of the evening tracking down these truants and bringing them back into the group. The next night the two left again. This time the staff did not chase about looking for them but, rather, went to the group and reported. "They really slicked you, didn't they?" This caught the group members off guard, and suddenly they were not at all sure just what the staff response might be to a truancy.

The effectiveness of planned unpredictability is seen in the great lengths to which youth will go to discover exactly what will happen if they engage in certain behavior. As a general guideline when students ask, "What will you do if . . . ," staff should not commit themselves to a specific response. Rather, all options are kept open with a general statement, such as "We'll have to see" or "There are several ways we could go on that." Thus, staff are not forced into a position where manipulative youth can predetermine their response.

The reader may wonder if this is a deceptive or unfair way to deal with people. In no circumstances should staff lie to young people or say they will do something that in reality they will not do. Yet often no useful purpose is served by laying out a specific blueprint of staff intentions. Staff should never be intentionally unfair, but since students have differing needs, staff responses to different youth cannot always be the same. The person who automatically metes out rigid consequences to every problem really is not being fair in providing for each individual's needs. But even if staff are not predictable, they do provide a basic consistency: All actions have the ultimate purpose of helping youth to grow toward responsibility.

THE GROUP-LEADER ROLE

The group leader plays a central role in the development of a positive peer culture. He is not a therapist in the usual sense of the word. Rather, his role is more that of a special kind of teacher or coach. He instructs, redirects, guides, and motivates but always makes the group responsible for working on problems. The group leader must be an effective limit-setter but also a sympathetic listener. Although he may convey an authoritative air, he does not relate to youth in an authoritarian manner.

The group leader's overriding purpose is to be helpful, and he does not allow himself to be entangled in battles with young people. He is very involved with his group but never presents himself in a manner that is ingratiating, condescending, or paternalistic. He is not trying to make the students dependent on him but instead works to develop the positive strength of the group.

The group leader understands that he must be able to work cooperatively with other staff members. Realizing that the students often will try to pit him against other adults or "the system," the effective leader never lets himself be drawn into actions that undercut fellow staff members. He has a unique role, since he is a party to the students' as well as the staff's confidential discussions. Therefore, he must be able to gain the trust and respect of youth and adults alike.

The group leader should have a stable personality and feel good enough about himself to be able to deal with others in a confident manner. He must be able to present himself as a warm, interested, and understanding person. He should not be afraid to show strong concern, because if he communicates only in a cold, intellectual style he will have difficulty in inspiring young people. The group leader should be firm and decisive, secure enough to admit mistakes, reevaluate situations from different perspectives, and adapt to changing circumstances.

He must be able to accept supervision but must not be overly dependent on others. He should be capable of exercising his own judgment and of operating with relative independence. He should not have excessive needs for approval or feel uncomfortable when he is required to take a position that others may regard unfavorably. While he should possess leadership skills and be able to inspire confidence in others, he must not be overly concerned with personal status.

The group leader's personal behavior must be beyond reproach. At no time should he give group members reason to say, "If he does it, why can't I?" He should feel comfortable in a variety of situations and be able to relate effectively with different types of individuals. He should not be struggling with his own issues of authority, for such conflict will severely hinder his ability to function as a strong, positive, adult authority figure.

The group leader must believe in people and their capacity for positive change and be convinced that people have a responsibility to one another. He must enjoy working with young people and be a person they want to become involved with. He should understand that the rewards may be few and the demands and frustrations many, and he should be sufficiently interested in the challenges of the position to extend himself beyond the routine working day.

The group leader must be able to project a model that will inspire youth to identify with him. This is a particular problem with many delinquent youth who have learned only to respect the powerful and the manipulative. With such youth, the group leader will need to be able to develop a kind of respect that borders on mystique. The primary basis of his mystique is that he is highly knowledgeable about all aspects of the group situation. He understands how each group member is really functioning, not just how each appears to be functioning. He is attuned to all interactions within his group, and he uses every source possible to keep himself fully informed on his group's status.

Members come to assume that the leader cannot be fooled. He appears to know what will happen before it actually does; he is able to predict the group members' behavior; but he is able to maintain for himself a position of unpredictability. He must be able to enter the thought processes of young people and to anticipate what they might be thinking or planning. Since much of his group members' behavior may be clandestine and secretive, he must become skillful at "deceiving the deceiver" [1] without becoming deceitful. At times, he must be able to keep his group off balance; but the members can always rely on the consistency of his concern.

The group leader does not adopt the group members' subcultural language or profanity but should be able to convey that he is in tune with their language and understands what they mean as they communicate with one another. Therefore, the group leader will become knowledgeable in cultural, ethnic, and colloquial expressions in order to avoid being perceived as "out of it" by the group members.

The group leader must always behave in a mature manner. He does not become involved in foolish horseplay with group members, knowing that such activity only erodes the group's respect for him as an adult. Similarly, he never relates his own youthful delinquent escapades, never tells off-color stories to the group members, never makes humorous references to the students' possible sexual activities, and never makes light of any of their problems. He maintains a certain formality in his relationship with students and refers to them by their given rather than their street names.

The leader does not see his role as that of an individual psychotherapist. He understands that to encourage students to bring their problems to him could undercut the group's effectiveness and so is careful that individual communications do not serve to isolate a particular student from the group process. He will, however, have individual contact with students outside of group meetings. Sometimes these interactions may be confrontive, as when he privately tells an individual that his behavior is unacceptable.* He may feed to certain group members information about another member who is deceiving the group. For example, he may reveal what really happened to a student on his last home visit rather than let him continue to deceive other members. He may also use private communication to challenge individual members to participate more fully in the group process or to support a youngster whose immediate needs cannot be met by the group alone.

*Redl and Wineman [2] referred to such encounters in their discussion of the life-space interview; they labeled these confrontations as "reality rub-ins."

The Group-Leader Role in Meetings

The PPC group leader plays a specific role in group meetings. He does not function in an authoritarian manner, but he is not uninvolved. Since the group members are expected to operate their own meetings, the group leader's role is to teach them procedures for running effective meetings and then to ensure that the members are performing successfully.

In the group meeting, the leader sits behind a desk and the group sits in a circle as in Fig. 7.5. This physical layout sets the tone of interaction. The leader is not a member of the group but is set apart in a position to influence the interaction as he deems necessary. In a well-established group, the leader makes few interruptions in the discussion until the final minutes of the meeting, when he summarizes the session.

A common mistake of beginning leaders is to be too passive or uninvolved. The passive leader is all but ignored by his group, has difficulty interjecting ideas, and sometimes sits on the sidelines as the group bogs down and becomes totally dysfunctional. Such a leader is much like a coach who throws out a basketball to a collection of people who have never before played the game and tells them, "Go to it." Some passive leaders have even gone so far as to change the seating arrangement so that the group sits in a circle and the leader sits outside it, which places the adult in a role where he is unable to provide effective leadership.

The opposite mistake of beginning leaders is to be overly active and dominating, a very common error, since most group leaders initially feel they must intervene and control the group when things go awry. In such

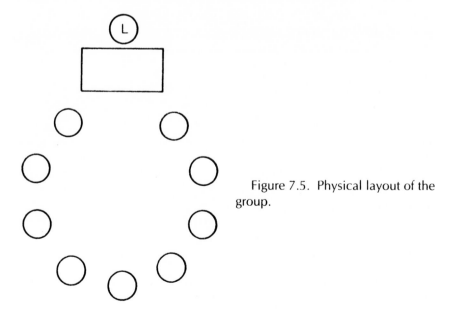

Figure 7.5. Physical layout of the group.

groups, the students continually orient toward the adult, who becomes like a schoolteacher conducting class: "Ron, what are your problems?" "Go ahead and speak up, Bill." "You two, back there, quiet down and pay attention." Or even, "Go ahead, you can speak without my permission." If the leader cannot lower his visibility, the group never will be able to develop its potential.

The leader's nonverbal behavior is particularly important in conducting group meetings. During the meeting, the leader generally will not show marked facial expressions but will quietly display interest in the proceedings. Any restlessness, boredom, shifts of posture, pointing, or eye contact will have the effect of orienting the group's attention away from the members and toward the leader. In initial stages, the members will constantly be looking to the leader for his reactions; therefore, he must be able to avoid giving nonverbal cues to his reactions, thoughts, or anxieties lest the group concentrate on him instead of the members' problems.

The group leader's primary verbal behavior is the question. The effective leader will learn many ways of asking brief, simple questions in order to direct or stimulate the group toward the solution of problems. For example, while several group members all talk simultaneously, a highly perceptive comment from one youth goes unnoticed. The group leader does not tell the group, "You shouldn't all be talking at once," or make any other directive comment. Rather, he only needs to ask, "Did the group hear Ronald's question?"

The use of questions has two major advantages: They are nonauthoritarian communications, and they force young people to learn by discovering the answers themselves. With a well-developed technique of questioning, it is possible (although not necessary) for the leader to frame all of his comments in this form throughout the entire meeting.

One way to determine whether a group leader is playing an appropriate role in the meeting is to note his and the members' use of pronouns.

You: If group members are continually using the word *you* in reference to the group leader, then they are converting the meeting into a two-way conversation with him. If the group leader frequently uses the pronoun *you* to address members, then he is setting himself up for such two-way communication. More neutral references are preferable: "Does the group see . . . " or "The group will probably want to . . . " or "When John has solved his problems he will . . . ." This form directs the group toward communication among its members.

I: The leader should avoid all self-directed comments, since they may cause the group to be overly concerned with pleasing the adult. Typical examples of this mistake are: "I was disappointed. . . ," "What did I say about that?", and "I was really glad to see. . . ."

We: The group leader should never use *we* or *us* when he really means the group. Thus he does not say "We were not very serious today" but "The group did not seem very serious today." The concept that must always be remembered is: *The group leader is not a member of the group. If he acts as if he were a member, then the group will not be able to develop full responsibility.*

A common confusion of role is seen when the leader tries to do the group's job by conducting individual therapy with the group as an audience. Sometimes he is not aware of his action and only by tape recording or observation can it be pointed out to him. For example, if the group is discussing a student's problem, the inexperienced group leader is strongly tempted to jump into the action, to begin asking the youth questions, or to make "insightful" interpretations to the individual. The new leader should follow the practice of never directly addressing the person who is the focus of the meeting. Rather, he should find some way of making his input through the other members. For example, he might ask, "Is the group interested in finding out why Garcia feels he always has to be high on drugs?"

The following questions, which a group leader asked in the span of 3 minutes, exemplify how one can be entangled in individual counseling within a group. "Do you understand what I mean?" "Can you explain, Amy?" "What did you do then?" "Who saw it happen?" "How did you feel?" After these questions, the group leader addressed a student, "Why are you looking to me? Ask the group." To any observer, it was quite obvious that the adult was making herself the center of attention. This leader was asking the members to solve their own problems, and yet all interaction worked against that goal.

Another problem of group leaders is an inability to keep quiet during the meeting. Frequently, the group builds up a head of steam and the leader interjects some observation. The members feel they have been interrupted, the meeting loses its impetus, and communication becomes disorganized. The leader must learn to intervene in a way that doesn't dampen the group process (unless he intends by his interruption to subdue an overly emotional group). He should not add trivial comments to the ongoing discussion; there is absolutely no need for him to vocalize the therapeutic "mm-hm" or to support the group's interaction by comments such as "that's right" or "good point" or "I agree." These interruptions distract the group and place the leader in a position where he seems to be competing to get a word in edgewise.

The group leader should always strive for maximum involvement of members. He is responsible for teaching youth to become effective helpers to one another.

Group-Leaders' Training

Successful group leaders have emerged from many kinds of backgrounds. No one profession appears to be more advantageous than another in producing effective leaders. Although formal training in human behavior is useful, many other variables seem equally or more important. In fact, some sensitive, concerned individuals with no formal educational background have become highly successful group leaders.

The use of two group leaders who alternate in conducting meetings or who serve simultaneously as coleaders is not recommended. Since the group leader becomes fully involved in the underlying process of his group, he develops his own style, perceptions, and central plan. If the group is forced to alternate between two leaders, inconsistencies develop that will have a negative effect on group cohesion. Experimentation involving two adults as coleaders of a group has revealed an increase in the level of adult control, which is contrary to the entire trust of a PPC program. The meeting belongs to the students, not to the staff, and the need for training group leaders should not be allowed to take precedence over the needs of the group.

Group-leader training should include a wide range of experiences. We must state most emphatically that one cannot become a leader just by reading a book. In addition, the trainee should have broad exposure to an operating PPC, should study the administration and organization of PPC programs, should analyze audio or video tapes of PPC groups, should observe groups at various stages of development, and should serve a supervised practicum or internship in conducting a group.

Even when the group leader has become experienced he should strive to increase his skill and effectiveness. One of the best ways for continuing inservice training is for leaders to conduct periodic observations and provide feedback to one another. The group leader who becomes overly comfortable or mechanical in his role is losing the opportunity for continued professional growth.

Substitutes and Trainees

If absolutely necessary, a strong positive group usually will be able to operate for a short time without regularly scheduled meetings. The substitution of group leaders will be detrimental, but if a leader must be absent for a long time, a substitute should be considered. The substitute should understand the structure and techniques of operating PPC groups and should have observed the particular group involved. Although the structured format of PPC groups makes substitution plausible, it should be avoided whenever possible.

Substitutes and trainees should be aware that some groups tend to stage release meetings, manipulate home visits, or test the limits in other ways in the absence of the regular leader. The substitute should not become overly involved; he should keep his distance, perhaps withholding most of his comments until near the end of the meeting. He should play a self-effacing role and avoid setting himself up as an expert, only to be shot down by the group. Often a group will feel that the new leader is inexperienced, is not interested in them, or may be unable to handle the strong emotion that could arise in the meeting. If he intervenes excessively in the meeting, the leader can become a target for mass hostility. Therefore, the trainee or substitute should work on the assumption that the students will be able to handle their meeting with minimal intervention.

NOTES

[1] Willie Hoffer, "Deceiving the Deceiver," in *Searchlights on Delinquency*, K. R. Eissler, ed. (New York: International Universities Press, 1949).
[2] Fritz Redl and David Wineman, *The Aggressive Child* (New York: The Free Press, 1957).

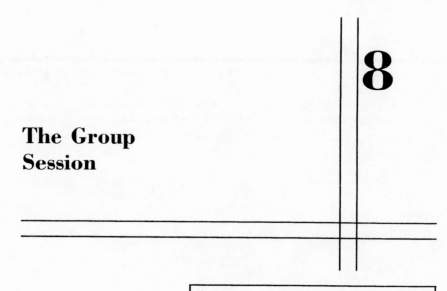

8

The Group
Session

THE FORMAT FOR MEETINGS

The Agenda

PPC group meetings follow a clear agenda that systematically involves all members and yet provides wide latitude for spontaneous individual expression. The meeting is not operated in a laissez-faire manner but is structured for efficient problem solving. The meeting consists of four distinct parts, but an established group moves so smoothly through the meeting that an untrained observer perhaps would not notice the overall plan.

1. *Reporting problems.* During the first part of the meeting, every member reports on the problems he has had since the last session as well as on other problems he has not yet brought to the group's attention. Each member is responsible for bringing out all problems in a clear yet brief manner, and if he omits any, other group members may call this lapse to his attention. The problem session varies in length but typically lasts 15 minutes.

2. *Awarding the meeting.* After all members have reported their problems, the group must decide who will "have the meeting." This decision is

based on who needs help most that day. After the members reach a consensus, they are ready to work with that one individual. Deciding who is to have the meeting generally takes about five minutes.

3. *Problem solving.* Here the group members concentrate on understanding and resolving one member's problems. If the group has been able to cover earlier steps efficiently, considerable time is available to work on problems. The problem-solving session typically lasts almost an hour and constitutes the major portion of the meeting.

4. *The summary.* Here the group leader engages in his most active role of the meeting. His summary of what has occurred teaches group members to become more effective in operating their meetings. The leader allows approximately 10 minutes for his summary.

Length of Meetings

PPC meetings usually operate for 90 minutes in treatment settings and for one class period in school-based programs. Shorter meetings make it difficult to adequately cover the various stages. For example, if problem reporting were omitted, the group would have no systematic method for reviewing problems in a manner that involved each member. Some may wonder whether a 90-minute session is excessively long. Anyone who has witnessed PPC groups in action soon finds this question answered. No properly operated meeting is boring, and the 90 minutes usually pass quickly.

Why, then, should the meeting be terminated at the scheduled closing time if the group is going well or appears about to open up a new problem? In contrast to the marathon-group notion, a PPC meeting always gives one the security of knowing an end is in sight. If some of the issues have not been fully resolved, they can be considered later. Of course, this firm closing sometimes leaves work for the group to do outside the meeting, but there is absolutely no need to achieve complete closure. In fact, the group leader often will close the meeting with several problems unresolved, leaving loose ends, and a member of a new group may ask, "Why are we quitting when we are just getting going?" The group leader can respond, "It will be interesting to see if the group's concern continues after the meeting." The group leader never creates the impression that he is indispensable or that the group cannot be trusted to help without his presence.

Sometimes new group leaders have a desire to shorten meetings that are not going particularly well. This move would be a serious mistake. If the group leader tends to adjust the length of the meeting, depending on how well the members are doing, then, in effect, by varying behavior the group is able to control the length of the meeting. The group may really be conditioning the leader: "We'll all act restless now, and then he will call the meeting to an end." If the group members want to quit and say they have no more problems to talk about, the group leader should reverse this situation by asking, "Does this mean that the group has solved all problems?"

Time of Meetings

Group meetings are held five times a week in treatment settings. If the group does not meet this regularly, it is questionable whether sufficient momentum to build and maintain a positive peer culture can be established. A less frequent meeting schedule is sometimes necessary in public school and community-based programs.

The question has sometimes been asked, "Couldn't the group meet fewer times a week and meet for a longer period of time?" Meetings that run longer than 90 minutes usually are not productive. Further, a continual, almost daily focus on resolving problems is lost if the group meets only three or four days a week.

In residential programs, evening meetings are ideal if the schedule will allow them. Usually the evening is a prime relaxation time, and by giving up that time the members are investing themselves. The question "How do you get them to meet in the evening?" is only raised by those who are new to PPC programs; once a positive culture is operating, youth will show more interest in their evening meetings than in sports, television programs, or similar activities. Another advantage of evening sessions is that students can reflect on the activity of the entire day. Further, evening meetings are not so likely to compete with other parts of the program, such as school or work programs. Finally, in evening meetings, most individuals relax, let down their guard, and speak more freely about themselves than they do during the hustle of the day. Ideally, public school groups meet near the end of the school day.

The Physical Layout

The group leader, seated behind a desk, indicates nonverbally how he should be viewed and how he will interact in the meeting. The group is seated in a circle that joins at the corners of the leader's desk. Members should sit in reasonably comfortable chairs (folding chairs are adequate) but not on couches, nor should they sprawl on the floor or meet outdoors on the grass; such postures detract from the serious, businesslike tone, and the members become overly comfortable. The appropriate tone is created as members sit in straight chairs, facing one another.

The issue of having a desk for the group leader merits comment. If the desk is removed, the entire psychological tone is changed. No longer is the adult "the leader" but now becomes a participant. While some new group leaders argue that they are more comfortable sitting in a circle, the purpose of the group is not to meet the needs of the adult. If the leader is in the circle he becomes the most competent member of the group, and the entire tone of the interactions reflect his presence. Further, such a physical arrangement makes it seem natural and legitimate for the group members to direct hostility toward him if they wish, thereby undercutting the authority position essential to certain interactions outside the meeting.

The many possible variations with which different group leaders have experimented all create an improper nonverbal tone. In order that the PPC group leader can avoid these pitfalls, Figure 8.1 diagrams seven ways not to arrange a group and, again, the proper layout for a PPC group.

The Tone of the Meeting

The group meeting is the core of a PPC program and, as such, the single most intensive activity the students engage in. The group leader strives to create an aura of serious importance for the meeting. Effective groups frequently approach the meeting in an almost sacred manner; horseplay, flippant behavior, and humor are alien to the task at hand. In every way possible, the leader strives to communicate (and must himself believe) that the meeting is of the utmost importance. As one youth in a PPC group said, "It's like going into surgery. We have someone's life in our hands."

No interruptions should be tolerated in a group meeting. Telephones should not be ringing, messages should not be delivered, people should not be moving in and out of the room. The room itself should be large enough to accommodate the group circle and should be well ventilated and quiet. Noise from adjacent areas should be minimal in order to avoid distractions, and conversation should not be audible outside the room. As most group leaders become experienced they even avoid taking notes during the meeting, since it may be distracting and may cause some of the students to feel that what they say is being transcribed.

The following example shows a group that violates the proper tone of a PPC meeting.

"We have someone's life in our hands"—PPC student

Boys came and went from the meetings as they pleased. In some cases their departure was to use the bathroom; in others it was to supply themselves with cookies and water. Discussion continued in spite of the activity or two playful dogs who not only tussled in the middle of the room but were constantly pawing a glass door to be let in and out. The telephone rang several times between 7:00 and 8:30. The meeting continued while the staff members even left the room for short periods of time. Boys from another group went by, stopped in the doorway to listen in. Curious adult staff wandered in and out as their schedules allowed. At one point in time six visitors were observing the procedures.*

The group leader also communicates the overriding importance of the session by doing everything in his power to avoid ever canceling a meeting, for this act would suggest that something else is more urgent. The group

*Personal communication, Oliver J. Keller.

(a) Around a circular table. The table is a barrier to communication and the group leader does not have the appropriate separateness.

(b) Around a rectangular table. Group members cannot readily see one another and the persons who occupy the end places are in positions of inordinate power and influence.

(c) A circle with the group leader sitting outside. The leader cannot even see half the members nor be seen by them. The group "belongs" so totally to the members that the leader is powerless in his attempts to influence it.

(d) A circle with a hot seat in the middle. Here the individual "having a group" sits (or even kneels) in the center. This places him in a highly vulnerable position, surrounded with no escape—not an arrangement for a group based on trust.

Figure 8.1. Variations in the physical layout of the group meeting.

80

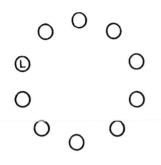

(e) A circle that includes the group leader. Here the adult functions as peer. He might be happier if he could find a friendly group of his own peers.

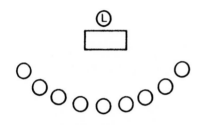

(f) A desk with the group in a broad semi-circle. The shape of the room and placement of the desk puts too much focus on the leader. Group members are so dispersed that those at the ends can scarcely communicate with others.

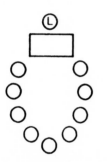

(g) A desk with the group in a horseshoe. Many members are too distant and those along the sides cannot see all of the others. The group leader and the member opposite the desk are in positions of inordinate control and influence.

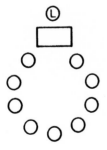

(h) Proper layout for a PPC group. The leader and all members can easily see one another. The leader is symbolically removed to place responsibility on the group and is in position to intervene when necessary.

Figure 8.1. *Continued.*

meeting should always start on time, and the leader should never make the group wait for him. If the adult expects the group to be prompt, then he must set the tone.

Before the meeting time, the students should enter the room and arrange the chairs or desks. The group leader should not set up the room for them, because this is their meeting and their responsibility. During the time before and after the meeting, the leader should avoid unnecessary exchanges. "Hi there, Teach!", "Can I make a phone call?", "Why is this visitor sitting in here today?" are interactions that suggest that the group is not ready for the serious consideration of problems; such a group may waste half the meeting before getting down to business.

During the session, students should feel free to express their real feelings and to use the language they are comfortable with as long as it does not hurt others. While there is no value in meetings that are characterized by members screaming profanities at one another for one and a half hours, the group leader should not be in the position of trying to control all of the members' verbalizations. "We don't talk like that in here," may be appropriate in a regular classroom but does not set the proper tone for a group meeting.

In order to determine whether to respond to profanity, the group leader should understand three different kinds of profanity:

1. Profanity as a response to intense frustration, physical pain, or emotional hurt may not be appropriate outside the group meeting but may well be ignored during the session.

2. Profanity to create an effect is seen when the individual seeks to build himself up or to attack others by employing emotionally charged language. If this becomes excessive the group leader may wish to call attention to what is happening, perhaps with a question such as "Does swearing make John feel like a big shot?"

3. Colloquial profanity is the habitual use of terms, which, while perhaps offensive to the general public, do not have emotionally charged meaning to the person employing them. For example, the term *bullshit* (meaning "dishonest communication") is a commonly accepted term in certain social groups, although it can be a highly charged word in other settings. The group leader may choose not to respond to colloquial profanity unless members are employing it in a manner that is inconsiderate to the sensitivities of others.

Group interaction may become so intense that all members are asking questions at once rather than coordinating their attempts to help the individual. The members must learn not to interrupt one another but to stick with the questioning until they get an answer to a problem. They should not continually jump from question to question just because the individual cannot immediately come up with an appropriate answer.

While no one can help if everyone is talking at once, still the group leader should not confuse a united and enthusiastic group with a disorderly one. The members should not be compelled to stand quietly in line waiting their turns. The feeling of the meeting as well as the content will carry the communication. A group with individual members all trying to help at once is far better than a quiet, boring, and sleepy meeting.

Confidentiality of the Group Meetings

The group must be convinced of the confidentiality of their meetings, and the members must learn that they do not have the right to reveal information to persons outside the group. In the early stages of group development, members will consider the discussion of problems as informing on one another, and a strong emphasis on confidentiality will be necessary if they are to overcome their reluctance to tattle on one another. The group must learn that talking about problems is helping and not informing.

When a group member reveals information in the meeting, he should not be punished for his revelation. For example, a student who reports that he has stolen something from the office should not be handled in a punitive manner. (If, however, a person failed to report this act "in group" and it was discovered through other sources, he would be subject to possible disciplinary measures.) Youth must be free to bring out their problems in the group without fear of social retribution from either staff or peers. They also should understand that as they talk about their problems they will be protected as much as possible from legal retribution.

Information derived from the meeting sometimes may be essential for treatment and thus may be available to other involved staff. The group leader himself must use considerable judgment in his dealings with other staff. He does not want to foster the impression that he is no longer a responsible colleague, but still, if he carries specific tales to others, he will soon undercut the group's trust in him. He has the considerable challenge of simultaneously building trust with both students and staff in a manner that is not dishonest to either.

As a climate of trust is established, certain "harmful" problems can be opened up without a feeling of threat. Perhaps the potency of the confidentiality issue can best be shown by the summary of the offenses (Table 8.1) committed by nine members of a positive peer group. The leader of this group listed the offenses known to the courts that referred the youths to the program and then listed the offenses that were revealed to the group but were not known to the court.

Recording Meetings

Since recordings may be useful for purposes of staff training, it may be permissible to tape-record or videotape the group meetings. Although not recommended as a regular and continuing procedure, in general taping is acceptable if it does not interfere with communication. If the group objects

Table 8.1. The Issue of Confidentiality: One Group's Revelations

Offenses known to court	Offenses not known to court, discussed in group
Student A. Petty larceny; brutality (holding 9-year-old boy over burning trash barrel)	Auto theft; breaking and entering
Student B. Beyond control of parent; sexual intercourse with 12-year-old sister	Auto theft; attempted rape; stealing; shoplifting; breaking and entering; vandalism; sexual acts with animals; incest with mother
Student C. Shoplifting; disorderly conduct; grand larceny; breaking and entering; destroying private property; truancy	Habituation to drugs; grand larceny; petty larceny; arson; auto theft; carrying concealed weapons
Student D. Curfew violation; auto theft; breaking and entering; public drunk; operating motor vehicle without license	Carrying deadly weapon; robbery; arson; auto theft; multiple breaking and entering; three instances assault and battery
Student E. Truancy; runaway; obtaining merchandise under false pretenses	Habituation to drugs; shoplifting; auto theft; vandalism; "rolling queers" for money (assault, battery, robbery)
Student F. Petty larceny; contempt of court; curfew violation; breaking and entering	Malicious cutting and wounding; housebreaking; stealing; forgery; shoplifting
Student G. Breaking and entering; attempted safe burglary; safe burglary	Carrying a deadly weapon; malicious cutting and wounding; burglary; concealing stolen property; fraud; stealing from automobiles
Student H. Shoplifting; runaway; violation of probation	Breaking and entering; stealing
Student I. Public intoxication; petty larceny; carrying concealed deadly weapon; burglary; attempted safecracking	Shoplifting; driving without license; breaking and entering

to being taped, the group leader should drop the issue for the time being. The group also should understand that if an individual feels his ability to be open about his problems is hampered, the taping will be discontinued. To do otherwise is to create hypocrisy about the importance and seriousness of the group meeting.

Taping should be done only under the closest controls and solely for the purpose of staff training or for orientation of persons seriously interested in the PPC program. Tapes generally should be played only if accompanied by discussion with someone who understands the process. Such analysis of the sessions is serious educational business and never should be allowed to become humorous entertainment. It should go without saying that groups should not be taped without their knowledge, for such action is a clear violation of the trust adults are asking youth to place in the group process. Playing their tapes as a learning process for the group is not advisable, since whatever feedback individuals need should be spontaneously provided by their peers or by the group leader.

Visitors in the Group

Periodically, it may be necessary to allow a visitor to observe a group meeting. The visitor usually will be a professional person with a serious interest in learning about the program.

The visitor should be oriented to the group procedures ahead of time. He should be instructed to sit at the back of the room and to avoid any interactions with the students (and the students are expected to regard the visitor as if he were not there). The visitor should not make eye contact with members of the group during the meeting, laugh, whisper, show any nonverbal reaction, or look disinterested. The visitor must commit himself to stay for the entire session, for his walking out midway through a meeting could be disruptive. He should never speak up at a meeting, and if he has questions or feels something should be clarified, he may talk with the group leader in private after the meeting. If a group member is awarded the meeting and feels uncomfortable with the visitor present, he should be permitted to ask him to leave; the visitor should be informed of this possibility before the meeting.

As a matter of general policy, visitors should not be family members or friends of students in the group. One exception would be a former member who returns to visit his old group, which is acceptable if the leader feels his presence will be helpful to current group members.

Any visitor must be approved by the group leader, who will decide if his group is ready to have a particular visitor. (The leader's supervisor is not considered a visitor and is always entitled to sit in on meetings.) The number of visitors in a group should be limited and should never exceed three or four at one time, otherwise a grandstand effect will be created. Some programs have facilities for visitors to observe from behind a one-way glass, but most PPC group leaders feel that students respond best when the visitor is seated in the room, since they believe that a person has the right to see who is observing him.

Visiting a group is one of the best ways of learning how a PPC program operates. However, as with surgery in a hospital, the observers are never allowed to interfere with the proceedings, since training must always be secondary to treatment.

REPORTING PROBLEMS

Reporting problems constitutes the initial stage of a formal group meeting and is designed to serve several important purposes. Each member's participation is structured from the outset so that no one is ever totally left out of interactions. As each member states his problems, he receives feedback on how peers see his behavior. Each individual has an opportunity to bring out problems himself rather than facing an "accusation" from group members. However, if a person omits some of his problems, the other members may point them out.

Problem reporting removes the communication barriers and feelings of distrust that often exist. As individuals relate their problems and discover that they are not punished, they become more open about their difficulties. This problem session allows members to get everything on the table so that each knows how all the others are doing. After reviewing all the problems of the day, they are in a better position to decide who should receive the meeting.

As the group reports problems, the leader can learn a great deal about the status of individual members. The problem session serves as an indicator of a student's honesty, commitment to solving problems, and concern for others. Since all members will speak up, the leader can quickly take the pulse of the entire group.

Beginning the Meeting

A mature group will be able to begin the meeting without any prompting or assistance from the group leader. The members will enter shortly before the scheduled meeting time and set their chairs in place. When everyone is present, including the leader, they begin to rotate around the group, reporting problems of the day. The group leader should not "start" the meeting, for this initiative conveys only that the members are there to perform for him. Neither should the group leader use the meeting for administrative matters, announcements, reading memos, or other such loose ends; this sets the wrong tone for beginning the meeting.

Students are expected to be at the meeting on time, but if they are late the group leader usually will not comment on the tardiness until he summarizes. If any members of the group do not arrive for the meeting but are known to be available in the area, it is the group's responsibility to find them and bring them to the meeting. The group leader should not do the group's job by trying to run down members who are not present. He needs only to note in his summary that certain members were missing and that those who were late were inconsiderate of the others who were ready to begin.

Occasionally, an entire beginning group skips a meeting. The group leader's general response is to remain in the meeting room, to occupy himself productively during the meeting time (e.g., by writing reports), and then to leave at the time when he would ordinarily summarize the meeting. If he tries to locate members or creates a confrontation about meeting attendance, he is communicating to the members that they have upset him. In fact, this is not the leader's but, rather, the students' meeting. Nevertheless, the leader and other staff should indirectly make use of the fact that the members did not show up and should make them appropriately anxious about their indifference to working on their problems. In these situations, members often are providing a direct test of the group leader. He must make this their problem and not his, communicating that he is available to do his job whenever the group is ready to assume its responsibility.

One other variation occasionally seen is the new group that arrives at the meeting room before the leader and (as another test) starts the meeting without him. Again, the leader does not act angry or threatened. Instead, he waits for some opportunity during the meeting to raise the issue in a serious but nonassaultive manner. For example:

> *Group leader:* Did everyone report their problems today?
> *Student:* Yes, you missed that because we started before you got here.
> *Group leader:* That raises some interesting questions about why some group members should be in such a hurry to get their meeting out of the way.

Concise Reporting

Problems should be presented as plainly and concisely as possible, using the Problem-Solving List vernacular for purposes of labeling. Sometimes a problem is presented so vaguely that it is not clear what the person is talking about; so each individual is expected to state the problem and then describe a specific incident. For example:

> *Student:* I was easily angered [*problem*]. One of my group members tried to tell me to be quiet in class, and I swore at him [*incident*].

If students state the incident without the problem or the problem without the incident, the group should act to clarify what is wanted. Initially, the group leader may teach students how to obtain clarification by asking, "Does the group understand the problem?" or "Did John tell the group what he means by an authority problem?"

Group members may become entangled in overdiagnosing a particular incident. A person reports an incident and then lengthily explains how the incident is an example of "inconsiderate of others," "authority problem," "easily angered," "easily misled," and so on. If group members get sidetracked in a discussion about the label a problem should have or in giving example after example of specific problems, then the leader teaches the group to streamline their communication. The leader may ask, "Does the group want Mary to keep explaining her problem to the group?" A group quickly learns to keep the reporting of problems clear and to the point.

Another confusion in the problem session arises when the group becomes bogged down in one person's problem and converts the problem-reporting session into a miniature problem-solving session. The group must learn to spot this diversion and redirect themselves. In teaching them, the group leader may ask, "Does John have the meeting now?" The group's negative answer will refocus the discussion on reporting problems.

In new groups, problem reporting may consume a very large portion of the meeting time and occasionally may even prompt the inexperienced group leader to suggest that the problem-reporting session be skipped. If this part of the meeting takes too long, the leader should discover the reason. Maybe the group is very much out of shape and really has so many problems that reporting them is a major project, but more likely the group has not learned to use the time well and is reporting trivial, meaningless problems. The group members may not yet be serious about helping and therefore are prone to waste time or engage in continual bickering.

The group leader will make the group sensitive to the extreme importance of effectively using all of the time for helping, since wasting time is really being inconsiderate of others. If students indicate that they have no problems to talk about that day, the group leader does not get into an argument with them. He may indicate that others see them as having problems, but if they need time to face up to their problems and find courage to begin dealing with them, staff are willing to wait.

To tell or not to tell.   A working group will see that all important problems are reviewed in the meeting, but when the culture is not strong the group will tolerate considerable bias in reporting. Students may not yet realize that pointing out problems can be helpful; instead, they view reporting as informing, which, of course, is a totally alien activity. The group leader must be sensitive about what is really happening beneath the surface verbalizations of such a group.

Through intimidation or through loyalty, a strong youth may hold such control over other group members that they are reluctant to bring up his problems. Conversely, a weak, unpopular member may suffer a barrage of accusations about all the problems others feel he has shown. At these times, the group leader should strategically place a question that calls attention to what is occurring. Even if the members are already aware of the dynamic, they see that he is monitoring what they are doing and is aware that they are not communicating openly.

Minimizing problems.   One way to avoid honest problem reporting is to minimize. A major problem may be described as if it were really nothing at all. If a youth has had a serious fight but reports only that "I was inconsiderate of Tony in our disagreement" then the group leader may ask, "Does the group understand what is meant by 'disagreement?'" A student may report that he has "a *small* fronting problem." If members do not note this minimization, the leader can ask, "Do problems come in sizes?" Likewise, such comments as "I *guess* I have a problem . . ." or "I have *sort of* an authority problem" are further attempts to minimize and might be countered with, "Does John have a problem or does John not have a problem?" An alert group quickly learns to detect and challenge these minimizations.

Overstating problems. Sometimes individuals are vying to get the meeting to an extent such that they overstate their problems. They may be seeking attention or may really want to solve their problems (perhaps in hope of being released from the group). In order that the youth who most needs the meeting will be identified, the group leader must function as a leveler of those who overstate (or understate) problems. In rare instances, a student may even create problems just to get a meeting, possibly choosing to "show a problem" just before the meeting begins. He may come to the meeting, slam the door, slide his chair back from the circle, sulk, and, in sum, radiate the message that he is bothered by something. The group must learn that using highly dramatic maneuvers does not guarantee that one will be selected to receive the group meeting for that day.

Denying problems. When a group member fails to report problems fully, his peers confront him with his lapse. The person often will acknowledge this reminder, but some individuals interpret the confrontation as "being criticized" and may refuse to acknowledge, possibly causing the problem session to deteriorate into a hot argument about whether or not the youth has a problem. The leader can redirect the group by asking, "Does the group see John as having this problem?" They usually will answer affirmatively; the point has been made, and they then can proceed to another issue. If the members feel strongly enough about the problem, they can give the youth the meeting so that the matter can be pursued in detail.

Projecting problems. As a student reports problems, he often tries to divert blame toward someone else. For example, a group member says, "I was easily angered by Mark's childish behavior." The group learns to spot this attempt to shift the focus away from the student's own problem. If the group does not recognize this maneuver, the group leader may ask, "Whose problem is being reported, anyway?" A member who is supposed to be reporting his problems has no business deflecting attention toward someone else; therefore, he cannot properly say, "Ed calls me names and picks on me, that's my problem for today" because he is really reporting someone else's problem, not his own. Group members learn to point out every example of putting problems off onto others, and in a working group no individual is allowed to dodge his responsibility.

AWARDING THE MEETING

The Process

After all group members have reported all their problems the group is ready to decide who will get the meeting. The process of decision making is as follows.

1. Each member of the group in turn is given an opportunity to indicate whether or not he wants the meeting, and if he does he states his reasons (e.g., "I want the meeting to work on my authority problem"). The group

then knows which members are requesting the meeting for that day.

2. Again in rotation around the group, each member makes a recommendation (not a vote) on the person he thinks needs the meeting most—possibly even someone who has not asked for the meeting. A typical interaction may be:

Student A: I think John should have the meeting to work on his authority problem.

Student B: I think Bill should have the meeting to work on his stealing problem.

Student C: I know Pete didn't ask for the meeting, but I think he should have it to work on his easily-angered problem.

3. After each member has made a nomination, several persons may be under consideration for the meeting. Group members continue the rotation process, giving the name of the person they want to have the meeting or changing their recommendation ("I want to change from John to Bill to work on Bill's stealing problem.") As an individual changes, he has only to say why his new nomination should have the meeting.

4. Usually by continuing the process of rotation, a well-functioning group will soon reach a consensus of who needs the meeting most. The decision must be unanimous, since a group split on who should be helped will not function as a cohesive unit. All members must be committed to help the youth who is awarded the meeting.

The Basis of Decision

One of the most important decisions a group makes is its choice of a person to receive the meeting, because that choice determines the course of the entire meeting. In reaching this decision, the group needs to keep in mind several questions.

1. *Who seems to need the meeting most?* In other words, who has the most serious problems, who has been showing the most problems, and what will be the effect on the person and others if he does not get the meeting?

2. *Who will use the meeting best?* If the group feels that a member will not effectively use the meeting and in fact resists getting it, they will have to consider these factors. Perhaps to give that member the meeting will not be a productive use of time. A group member should never expect, though, that just by his saying that he doesn't want the meeting, the group will back off and give it to someone else. If he is presenting clear problems, the group may well decide that they want to help him even if he is not asking for the meeting.

3. *How long since the person has had the meeting?* An individual may not have had a group meeting for a long period of time. Even though his problems may not be intense, he certainly should not be continually deprived of the meeting. Otherwise, persons with fewer problems or those

whose problems are not so destructive would never get help. The group must realize that all members need opportunities to resolve their problems in a group meeting.

4. *How hard is a person fighting to get the meeting?* Even if an individual has requested a meeting the group will want to assess how much he really wants it. Sometimes members request the meeting with less than a total commitment to work on their problems.

Awarding a meeting can be a very difficult decision, since the group must choose to focus on one individual; hence, members must be aware of the consequences of their choice. They are also responsible for supporting persons who do not get the meeting until they have the opportunity of getting one.

It should be noted that just because a student has been creating difficulties all day long (and often not accepting help with these problems), there is no reason to assume he will use the meeting well, and he will not automatically get the meeting. However, there is no reason to say that he cannot use the meeting, either. As the group often decides to give the meeting to the person who is showing the most serious problems, one individual may monopolize many meetings. The group must avoid a pattern of giving meetings predominately to only one person.

If a student with a serious problem does not get the meeting, the others often say, "We'll take care of it outside the group." While certainly they will need to help the student outside the group, if in fact he does have a serious problem, he must come to the group on another day to solve that problem. It is assumed that such a student will continue to ask until he is awarded the meeting.

There is no set limit on the frequency with which one person can get the meeting, and the group leader should not make arbitrary rules such as, "No two meetings in a row." The leader should also be aware of the tendency for groups to try to schedule who is to get the meeting in advance, which is not acceptable; a sound decision can be made only on the basis of thoughtful consideration of all available information.

The Search for Consensus

The struggle to reach a decision on who needs the meeting can be animated and at times frustrating. Group leaders may become upset at the difficulty a group sometimes has in reaching a consensus. They need not always be concerned, since having several members vie for a meeting can be a healthy process. There may be honest differences of opinion on who most needs the meeting, but differences can also cause a power struggle among individuals not really interested in deciding whose need for help is greatest. The new group leader tends to become anxious when a group bogs down and cannot agree on awarding the meeting, but he should view such an impasse as a good diagnostic tool that allows him to see what patterns of support emerge. The conflict need not be solved for them, because an inability to decide who to help indicates they probably are not in very good shape to offer help. Occasionally, the leader may even let the group spend a whole meeting in trying to decide who should be helped, which may be a trying experience for a group but may also stimulate members to try to "get it together."

There is one exception to the expectation of unanimity of consensus on the part of the group. If one individual acting out of negative stubborness tries to sabotage the meeting by refusing to join with the others who have agreed to give the meeting to an individual, the group leader may neutralize him. The leader may ask: "Does the group feel they have sufficiently discussed all the reasons why John should have the meeting today?" When the group answers affirmatively, the group leader may then ask, "Is the holdout using his power to help or hurt?" "To hurt," is the answer. "Then why are you letting him hurt the person who needs the meeting?"

It should be added, however, that in some circumstances the group leader may choose not to intervene to rescue the group from one member who is holding out. Perhaps they need to learn to deal with his stubborn resistance. If one person is willing to keep others from geting help, then he may be showing (whether he realizes it or not) how much he needs the meeting himself.

The group leader must learn the subtle process of influencing the group without controlling it. In no case should he ever nominate a member to receive the meeting, because he then makes the meeting the leader's "property," which will undercut the group. The leader must hold the group accountable for making a good decision. When the group has reached consensus on who should receive the meeting, they are then able to begin work on problems.

PROBLEM SOLVING

When a group is strong and positive, the members demonstrate great skill in helping the student who gets the meeting to understand and work toward a resolution of his problems. However, working groups do not develop automatically. The group leader must do a great amount of teaching to develop and maintain the group as an effective helping agent. As in the problem session, the leader attempts to limit most of his participation to questions, avoiding authoritarian interventions. In a working group, the leader has to make only a few interventions during the course of the meeting, and those he makes must not undercut the group's own responsibility to run the meeting.

When a group leader intervenes, he should not do so in a wordy, complex manner. If a group is not asking the right questions in order to bring out problems, the leader may ask, "Does the group know what Susan meant when she said she is rotten?" The beginning leader usually has great difficulty in avoiding the temptation to play the role of therapist. Since the students are not yet able to function effectively, it seems natural for the leader to jump in and perform for them. This only increases the amount of adult involvement, which interferes with the development of a strong working group. The group leader must continually remind himself that he is not the group therapist but, rather, the coach, teacher, and supervisor of youth who must learn to master the helping process themselves.

In the beginning, the group will be quite willing to let the leader play a dominant role. If the leader notices that the students continue to look to him, he should divert their attention by turning to another member of the group, perhaps a nontalker. Through such use of eye contact, the leader can do much to keep individuals from continually turning to him for help.

Getting on the Track

As the group begins to work on problems, it initially makes many mistakes. The group leader strategically places questions, teaching the students to concentrate on clear and relevant communication. For example, if a student suddenly begins to dwell on the past, the leader should help the group to understand they cannot change the past but should concentrate on today's problems.

Frequently, the beginning group will seemingly lose the entire train of thought and wander to another topic; then the group leader may have to redirect them with a question, "What is the problem the group is working on?" If the group strays from the person who has the meeting, the leader evaluates whether the topic is important to the group; if it is not, he asks, "What does this have to do with Tom?" or "Who has the meeting?"

Giving the Meeting Away

Mike turned from talking about his problems by claiming he was upset because nobody else in the group cared about him. Why should others tell him what he should do to solve his problems while they had worse problems? Everyone was prejudiced against him. He could not trust anybody. At this point the others became rather defensive, trying to disprove all of Mike's allegations. The group leader intervened, asking "What has Mike just done to the group?" One of the members was able to point out that Mike was trying to give the meeting away to someone else.

If one of the students asks the group leader an irrelevant question, it should not be answered. The leader is responsible for teaching the group to deal with real and meaningful material. Some discussion of "dumb issues" is to be expected in the early stages of the group, since the students will not be trusting enough to get into serious matters. However, even established groups can become bogged down in "picky" discussions that inflate small and meaningless problems out of proportion.

For example, if members waste a lot of time in discussing whether a student has an authority problem because he won't use his fork properly, the meaninglessness of the discussion should be marked. If a youth somehow feels that he has all the 12 problems on the list, he will become demoralized, feeling he has no hope of ever resolving all his problems. The group leader must help to tie the group into the problems that are crucial to his progress.

This new group will look for superficial solutions. As soon as a person acknowledges his problems, the group will want to wrap it up by providing little sermons on his changing his ways, and then they will think the problem is solved. Frequently, the student will play into this easy solution by willingly agreeing to change, which then is supposed to bring the discussion to an end. The group must learn over a period of time that simple and superficial solutions may not suffice, that they are solving only incidents and not real problems.

Any group can easily become mechanical; therefore, the meeting should always be a dialogue and not just an exchange of old phrases. The group leader will carefully watch the group idiom and look for words that have lost clear meaning; then these words should be questioned, to be sure that the students are really communicating with one another. Sometimes the problems being discussed seem unrelated to real-life problems. Here, again, the leader should help the members to see a connection between the topic being discussed and the patterns of problems in the person's life. For example, the question "How does Mary's easily-misled problem get her into trouble in the community?" helps to relate present problems to broader past and future problems.

During the initial stages, the group may try to project their problems onto the leader. An example is the following:

> The group told John he had a drinking problem. John told the group, "Adults drink too," and then turned to the group leader, asking, "How about you, sir, do you drink?" The group leader did not answer, and an animated discussion ensued in which the group divided into two camps. One joined with John in attacking the leader and demanding that he answer the question; the other pointed out that the question was an attempt to put off the problem onto someone else. The leader sat expressionless through 5 or 10 minutes of argument until the group was polarized. Then, when he asked, "What did John just do?" the group was able to analyze John's maneuver. The group leader supported John in a sense and challenged the group by saying, "Smooth move. John almost got the group off himself." He then helped the group to recognize that they could not let John "slick them" if they wanted to help him with his problems.

The leader often is hard pressed to handle himself in a professional manner while his group attacks him. Nevertheless, he must not be lured into a defensive stance. The group's responsibility is to stop such a diversionary attack, and a leader must never do battle on the students' terms or turf. If nothing else, he can sit in silence or can counter with some bland comment such as "Could be" or "Oh." Sometimes a colorless and neutral response defuses the attempt to overpower the leader.

The group leader should avoid any questions designed to entrap him. If the group turns to the leader and asks, "What do you think?", the leader does not respond. A new group is likely to further challenge the leader by saying something like, "Well, how are we supposed to work on our problems if you won't even help us?" or "You don't even care about us; that's why you're not answering." The leader should patiently wait out these episodes, maintaining consistently that the group should be able to answer the questions. If the members try to involve the leader in an argument, a good technique is to divert the discussion back to the group by asking a question (e.g., "What does the group think about what Maria has just said?").

Another way of resisting the group leader is to ignore his comments. If the group does not respond to his question, he keeps going back to it in a persistent but nonthreatening manner, perhaps posing a further question about why the group is trying to escape the question. The leader should not wait for his summary to point out that they are ignoring him.

Detecting Rigged Meetings

The group leader must never assume that what appears to be happening in the meeting is what really is happening. Rather, he must always be somewhat careful and even suspicious of his group. He must stay on top of the group and be continually alert to any signs of hidden processes at work.

The most dramatic examples of group deception are rigged meetings, which are really fronts to cover up something. A member of the group may appear very angry with another member. If side glances and a smile accompany the anger, a con game probably is in process. Some of the signs of a rigged meeting are the following.

1. A student in the meeting suddenly becomes verbal after a long period of little or no interest in the group.
2. The attention of the group is placed on one or two scapegoats, and other students do not bring up their problems.
3. A student who has been "bad" for several months suddenly becomes "good." (A youth may feel that if he puts on a bad act for awhile and then follows with a good act, people will think he has changed.)
4. Students are playing up to either the group leader or other staff.
5. A student attempts to give information about other students on an individual basis rather than in a group.
6. Group members play it safe in the meeting, trying to keep anyone from getting angry.

Sometimes group leaders play into the problem of rigged meetings by wanting continuously pleasant group meetings. However, a good leader knows that group meetings cannot be permanently harmonious, that peace is a phase in the group's cycle. It is not desirable for the group always to remain on an even keel.

Reading Nonverbal Behavior

The group leader who is aware of nonverbal communication within the group has available additional information about what is really happening in group interactions. Nonverbal communication can occur in many different forms.

Appearance: Sloppy, proud, alert, depressed, unusual clothing, tattoos

Posture: Relaxed, tensed, disorganized, withdrawn, or challenging postures

Location: Proximity of students to one another and to group leader, noticeable body contact between students, seating arrangement, location relative to group (e.g., sliding chair a bit out of the circle)

Gestures: Movements of hands, nods of head, pointing, restless motions

Eye contact: Eye and head orientation, trying to hide face, glancing in suspicious ways, avoiding eye contact or looking away

Facial expressions: Signs of interest, involvement, or distress, change of affect, perspiring, blushing, twitching, grimacing

Nonverbal aspects of speech: Pitch, timing, rapidity, interruption, halting speech, stuttering

Protecting Members

An important group leader task is the protection of individual members from hurt by the group process. The leader must assess the group's ability to use deeply personal and confidential information in a helpful way, and when, on occasion, he feels that the group is not capable of this help, he must act to prevent a youth from exposing himself to the group.

> Tony looked extremely tense and told the group he had something he had to get off his chest. He then began to describe what appeared to be an episode of incest with his mother, but when the group members became aware of his subject two or three of them exchanged glances and giggles. The group leader noted the exchanges, realized the group was not in a position to help Tony with this matter, and so shut off the very important material before the youth had opened himself up to a group not ready to help. The group leader's simple move was to ask, "Would Tony tell the group about how he got along in junior high school?"

Sometimes it may be necessary for the group leader to shut off very important material that begins to emerge too late in the group session to allow enough time for members to hear the entire matter and adequately work through feelings. Here the leader intervenes in such a way that members can look forward to taking up the problem in some future meeting when more time is available for discussion.

Group members occasionally try to hurt one another in a meeting, either psychologically or physically. These attempts will occur within a group that is not yet positive; thus, during interrogation of a youth, someone may become so frustrated that he uses epithets. If the group does not stop this hostility, the group leader must, usually with a question like "How is that helping?" A youth may also make some gesture that implies physical intimidation. The leader must be alert enough to intervene before actual physical abuse occurs.

If the group leader is unequivocal in his rejection of hurting interactions, there is very little chance of a serious fight in a meeting of an established group. The leader must teach the group that if a person gets angry and loses control, the response of others will be to help him and not to reciprocate anger. However, a working group is sensitive enough to know when someone may be hurt, and in such a group the young people themselves can help to play the protective role.

Life Story

A variation of the usual problem-solving meeting is the life story. A student will tell his life story at a group meeting that he requests for this purpose. The life story is really a social history through the youth's eyes. Going back as far as he can recall, he recounts his relationship with family, peers, school, and community, and tells all the problems he has had, including those that others may not know about. He is allowed to bring out, without undue criticism from the group, what he thinks is important. A new youth relating his background often brags about his escapades and accomplishments. His peers watch and "diagnose" him, since many defense mechanisms are revealed in these first sessions.

Particular emphasis is placed on the parts of a person's life story that relate directly to current problems. The group leader initially may have to prompt discussion, but with experience a group will be able to elicit the life story in a comprehensive fashion. If a person does not bring up all the important details the first time, the assumption is that he will talk more freely when he is ready. Generally, a student will not tell his life story until he has been in the group a couple of weeks or more and until other members have had the opportunity to relate their life stories to him.

When the student has told his life story, the group then assigns problems based on the story. Possibly only at this time will the focus of the group be on the past rather than on the present or future; hence, the group leader may want to bring out and mark specific points for the group's attention in order to make clear the goals for the individual and the group. As members have further contact with the youth, they may at a later time assign other problems for the youth to resolve.

Discovering the Basic Problem

Some counseling theories are based on the idea that given an opportunity to express real feelings, a person will reveal the truth. Experience with many young people suggests, however, that one cannot be totally nondirective and still hope to discover what is really troubling a person. Well-developed defenses will not always be lowered unless the helping agent takes an active role in the communication. A working group does not wait interminably for a person to abandon his excuses. Instead, once a basic climate of trust has been created, group members become active in pointing out the implausibility of the account the youth is advancing.

As a young person is able to abandon defensive explanations, he becomes free to express honest feelings. Groups must learn to recognize all kinds of diversionary maneuvers so that ultimately they can help the individual to reach the truth. This process is in many respects well characterized by Conan Doyle's classic statement: "When you have eliminated the impossible, whatever remains, however improbable, must be the truth" [1].

An example will serve to clarify. A common problem in many groups is drug abuse, which in general is not interpreted as some special phenomenon totally separate from a person's other problems. (We are not talking here about a case of physical addiction but rather of psychological dependence. If a youth is physically addicted to drugs, then medical expertise should be sought to manage the physical problems associated with withdrawal.) Drug abuse usually reflects more basic problems in the person's life. As a group begins to work with this person, he will advance a number of seemingly plausible explanations. (1) It's really not a problem; I can stop any time I want. (2) I just do it because my friends do. (3) Research says drugs are not harmful. (4) All adults use drugs, like tobacco and alcohol. (5) I just want to enjoy myself. What's wrong with that? (6) It's my life; I can do what I want with it. The group must probe beneath these comments and pursue the questioning until they discover just why the person needs to use drugs. Often this investigation reveals a completely different problem. The youth may have such a poor opinion of himself that he is forced to follow others regardless of what they are doing. He may be so overwhelmed by feelings of conflict or inadequacy that he wants to get away, and drugs provide this escape. He may be uncomfortable in social interactions and use drugs to overcome the handicap (a common problem among adults who need a drink to loosen up so they can be good company). He may be only casually experimenting but trying to create the impression that he is highly sophisticated in drugs because he thinks he will gain status. He may be taking drugs to prove his independence from his parents. In some cases, he may be playing out some suicidal game in which he really would just as soon destroy himself. He may even be involved in the drug culture primarily for purposes of profit. Because of the number of possibilities, it is important that the group learn to carefully check out a person's story, continuing to ask questions until they reach the heart of the matter. One can best achieve basic change as one understands the basic problem.

Challenges in the Group Process

Group leaders confront many important issues as they strive to build the group into an efficient problem-solving unit. Let us consider some of them.

One of the more common problems is to secure the involvement of all group members. Most groups have at least one member who is largely a nonparticipant. The group leader usually will try to direct some interaction toward such a member, and he can recognize and praise any of the youth's contributions; many times, nonparticipants really are afraid they will say something wrong. Working to involve the silent member can cause considerable frustration among group members. Sometimes a member stubbornly refuses to answer even simple questions, which, unless the group is strong, is extremely frustrating and can precipitate an attack on the silent member: "Let's get him mad. Go ahead and get mad, lose your temper!" Such provocative games are not helping, and if a group member does not interrupt them, the leader should intervene by questioning what the group is trying to do.

Occasionally, a student resists communication about his problems by claiming that although he knows he has problems, he can handle them himself without the group's help. While the group usually will point out that he has not been succeeding very well, his argument is difficult for the group to counter. The group leader may want to teach the group strategies, such as the following:

- Is John saying that accepting help from others makes him feel small? Are some people not big enough to admit they could use help from someone else?
- Is John saying the group isn't good enough to help him with his problems?
- Is John saying his problems are too big for the group to be able to handle?
- If John is saying he doesn't need help, does he mean he will be unwilling to help others?

These responses will tend to place the student in a bind if he continues to resist the helping process.

Often a highly verbal member will lead the group along lines of his own interest, which, of course, precludes the involvement of others. Here the group leader can redirect with a question such as, "How many members are in the group?" The leader must be aware of the reason only one person is active in discussion; sometimes no others dare confront the youth who has the meeting, or no other members are interested in helping. In any event, this situation signals a serious problem with group functioning.

A variation of this problem is seen in the "two-man con game" in which two individuals carry on a conversation while the others sit idly by. For example, a lieutenant may be gingerly confronting the peer leader about a problem, taking extreme care not to say anything offensive and to shield the peer leader from strong confrontation, thus minimizing pressure and discomfort. Whenever interaction is limited to a small number of members, the group leader should be suspicious about what may really be happening.

Sometimes in talking about problems, a student will exaggerate or elaborate so as to create "war stories." The group leader must be alert to be sure the group is not joining in fantasy as the individual recounts tales of daring (delinquency, drugs, sexual and aggressive exploits). If the youth so describes situations that other group members receive vicarious satisfaction, the leader may intervene in the process by asking, "Is John trying to make his troubles sound exciting?" which should suggest to the group what is happening.

A common role in almost all groups is that of clown—the student who makes light of problems and seeks attention by acting clever and funny. The group leader places responsibility on both the individual and the group: "Why does John want to play the clown?" or "Why does the group let John play the clown?" or "What is John trying to cover up?" Such questions help the group members to avoid being controlled by the clown's humor.

Some students are sympathy seekers. If the group leader feels that an individual is talking about his problem in such a way as to gain sympathy from the group, he can easily handle the situation with the question, "Does John want the group to feel sorry for him?" Frequently, the group has a bully who is able to so intimidate the members that no one will bring up his problems. The leader can ask, "Why doesn't the group talk about Tom more? Hasn't he any problems?" or "Why does the group let Tom push them around?" Sometimes a youth's threatening gesture, comment, or tone of voice can intimidate those who are trying to help him. These signals tell the group members to back off. Comments such as "Don't you talk to me like that" or "I wouldn't say that if I were you" or "We'll settle this later" suggest an intimidation problem. Likewise, if the smaller members of the group are silent while a larger or more aggressive member is being discussed, the group leader may question: "Has anyone wondered why the smaller members of the group aren't helping? It can't be that they aren't smart enough; perhaps they are afraid to speak out. Can Tom get help if nobody dares to be honest with him?

Sometimes the group leader can neutralize an intimidating member by noting his behavior and predicting possible outcomes.

Joe seldom allows anyone to confront him; so when the group began to discuss his problem it seemed likely they would back off. At this point the leader said, "The group is now dealing with Joe and it will be interesting to see if the members become afraid of him or if Joe will get mad and show his temper problem, or if he will withdraw and sulk.

This is the technique of *predicting possible outcomes,* which when properly used has the effect of placing the youth in a bind where he would "lose" by trying any of his usual defensive strategies.

Sometimes the strongest, most sophisticated member of the group so masters group techniques that he becomes virtually impregnable to help from his peers. Then the leader must point out that even though he can help others, he is really not strong enough to accept help with his own problems. Group members may become anxious when confrontation is directed toward a strong member. They try to get others to back off, with comments such as, "Let's not get hostile," "Don't raise your voice," "Why do you keep asking him the same questions?" "Can't you see you are getting him angry?" These statements cue the group leader that members have not yet developed sufficient strength to face the strongest of their number.

Since many youth with problems are highly practiced at deception, it is possible that they will make a game out of the group meeting. They will put on an act, pretending to be concerned, while in reality they are not. If the group is well established and the fronter has been in the group for awhile, other students should note the deception. Also, the group leader can ask, "Does the group think Ron is really serious?" "Is he sneaky like that with all authority; is this how he worked his parents?" or some similar question that calls attention to the fraudulent nature of the communications.

A youth who enters a PPC program with prior group experience presents a particular problem. The student may initially be rather afraid of exposure and may distrust the group, or he may have learned well how to manipulate the group. Although the group usually knows such a new member is playing a role, weeks or even months may pass before they can outmaneuver this sophisticated youth. When his game is revealed, he experiences frustration and begins to act out, which is no cause for alarm but signals a new opportunity to begin again without game playing.

On occasion, a negative member will purposely try to destroy a group meeting. The following is an account of such a meeting.

Tonight Ron continually tried to destroy the meeting. He was so negative that he completely disrupted any possible progress. In a period of five minutes he made the following remarks: (a) I can fuck up this meeting anytime I want to. (b) I think we should give today's meeting to Davey, because he is a motherfucker. (c) I think we should give the meeting to Mr. Sheridan [group leader] because he needs our help. (d) I think we should give the meeting to Tony because he is an S.O.B. The group leader can get help some other time. (e) I want to change. I'll give it to Mark, because he's a mental case.

The group leader in such a meeting is in a very frustrating position. His natural inclination is to use his authority to confront the student, but if he does, he removes from the group the responsibility to manage the youth.

While no guideline can be given to meet every occasion, the group leader generally employs a reversal. He might question what the person is trying to accomplish, and in summary might comment, "Yes, it's hard to work on problems. Sometimes people don't feel they are adequate enough to face their problems, but the group will have plenty of opportunity in the future to help Ron."

Toward a Positive Self-Image

The foregoing discussion has included so many examples of possible complications in the meeting that the reader may get the impression the group leader faces a continual chain of disruptions. Such is not the case. In a working group, it is not at all uncommon for a leader to intervene as few as a half-dozen times in the entire course of the meeting. A new group will show many of the problems discussed, but an established group can handle most challenges with minimal adult intervention.

There is, however, one particular problem that many groups have difficulty in discussing, analyzing, and resolving—the problem of a low self-image. The group leader must always keep in mind that the primary resolution of a negative self-image problem comes not from discussion but from action. Nevertheless, regardless of the specific problem under consideration, the discussion often leads to the existence of an underlying self-concept problem. For example, the group may begin to work on a youth's authority problem but soon notice that he gets upset when other people tell him what to do, and they wonder how criticisms or directions can bother a person if he really feels good about himself. However, when the group gets to the self-image problem, they may not know just how to proceed. They have established that the person has a low self-image, but then they can think only of giving a pep talk or telling him to try harder or perhaps saying "I know, I'm that way too."

The following are typical questions the group leader can use in teaching the group to pursue problems related to a poor self-image:

1. *What is it that the person feels is so bad about himself?* Is it that he is stupid, that nobody loves him, that he is ashamed of how he looks, that he fears he is crazy or sexually inadequate, or what?

2. *What situations make him feel small about himself?* Is it failure, or being criticized, or being in competitive situations, or is it in relationships with parents or teachers or the opposite sex, or does he feel this way even when nobody is around?

3. *Who really makes him feel small about himself?* Can anyone make him feel small, can anyone succeed at putting him down if he really feels

good about himself, does he make other people's problems into his own by responding to their hostility?

4. *Whatever he thinks of himself, what is really the truth about him?* Is he really as bad as he fears, or as good as he pretends, is he trying to be more than it is possible for him to be, does he know his limitations? (A physically handicapped person in a wheelchair can feel good about himself if he works in a realistic way within his limitations.)

5. *What can he do to improve himself?* Does he give up easily or not try difficult tasks because he is afraid of failing, does he accept help, does he use to good advantage any opportunities to help himself?

6. *What does he do about the things that cannot be changed?* Is he going to keep feeling sorry for himself, is he going to give up, is he going to take it out on others, or can he accept himself for what he is?

7. *What are his strengths?* Has he helped the other members of the group, how can he feel good about himself, how has he solved the problems he had, how can the group help him to see that in his own special way he can be a great person?

As young people learn to master their difficulties and be of value to one another they come to view themselves as worthwhile. Understanding their strengths as well as their limitations, they are now able to live more effectively with themselves and others.

THE SUMMARY

During the meeting the group leader unobtrusively keeps time, leaving perhaps 5–10 minutes at the end for summary. At a point of his choosing, he stops the discussion by saying, "Time for summary." The leader himself should always call summary time. Occasionally, one member, perhaps noting that the leader always terminates the meeting exactly 10 minutes early, might say, "Summary time." Here the leader would do well to ignore the comment for a couple of minutes and delay the beginning of his summary, and vary his future timing more to ensure that members are not watching the clock to see when the summary begins.

During the summary, the group leader should remain seated, conveying a friendly but serious, relaxed but controlled tone. The summary of the meeting is not meant to be a diagnostic statement of the member's problem; the overriding purpose is to provide feedback to the group on how they performed in helping one another so they may become even more effective in the future.

The group leader should not fall into constant and predictable patterns but should use the summary time in as creative a way as possible. If he always conducts the summaries according to the same format, the group will be able to predict what is coming and will pay less attention. One summary may concentrate on how each individual person has helped; another may concern the person who had the meeting. On still another day a major portion of the summary may be devoted to discussions of issues that will become important only after the members leave the meeting.

The group leader can pose questions that involve students as a part of the summary, thereby making them feel important and pointing out what they learned during the meeting. Through this device, the leader can give credit to the members; as youth describe what happened, the leader can provide reinforcement for their insight and recall. Still, the leader maintains control of the overall summary; he does not delegate his responsibility by saying "John, you summarize the meeting today." Generally, the ratio of group leader/group member participation should be on a 60/40% basis. When the leader asks questions, he should phrase them so that someone in the group will be able to answer, but he should keep discussion confined to the topic at hand and avoid allowing another meeting to start during the summary.

The summary should not deteriorate into negative criticisms. This is not the format for moralizing or verbal spanking. Many new leaders find it much easier to criticize the members' performances than to call attention to their achievements. The leader can help the members to learn something even if the meeting did not go so well as it might have. He can help them to see what the meeting told them about each other, and he can refer to topics that still need discussion, since what was not said may be just as important as what was said. For example, "Some seem to feel that John did not say what really is bothering him. What does this tell the group about John?"

If a meeting is very lethargic, the leader may well use the summary to raise the group's anxiety. Thus, if he feels the group is not really working on problems, he may point out that one member has held something back from the group—but he will not name that member. Although at times it may be good to instill in group members anxiety about their performance, it is generally not good to leave a group in a frustrated state. The meeting may raise many emotions, and the group leader must, so to speak, close the wounds so the members may be able to function in a reasonable manner. If a group is frustrated over its inability to handle a difficult student, the leader takes the edge off the tension or hostility, perhaps with such comments as:

- "When the group learns to know John better, they will be able to help him understand his problem."
- "When John is able to trust more, then the group will be able to help him."
- "It is really amazing that even though John did not want any group members to help him with his problems, the group showed so much patience and understanding. It is obvious that they care enough about John to be able to help him in the future."

The summary can be used to build toward future challenges. The leader does not need to provide closure on every issue. If he wants to motivate the group toward a specific goal, he may purposely leave loose ends at the end of the meeting. Sometimes the leader raises a question for which the answer is not readily apparent: "Now that the group has learned that John is thinking of running away from here, one wonders whether the group will care enough about him to see that he doesn't hurt himself." Selective use of this powerful technique, *withholding closure,* can motivate the group toward some specific goal.*

As far as possible, the group leader should arrange for the group to leave the meeting with the feeling that they are or can be a helping team. Typically, he ends on a positive note, saying "Good meeting" or "Fine, that's all." The group then should leave the room; after the meeting is not a time for camaraderie beween the group leader and the group or for individual conferences. The leader does not answer such questions as "How did I do?" but redirects them to the group by saying, "You will want to ask your group that question." This keeps the tone serious and keeps responsibility on the group.†

DISCUSSIONS OUTSIDE THE MEETING

In a positive, helpful group, concern with problems is not limited to the group session but extends to life beyond the meeting. The intensive discussions in the meeting generate further reactions as students move to other areas of the program. Among the many potential reactions noted frequently after a group meeting are the following.

Negative: A sense of relief that the meeting has ended; feeling angry or upset about the inferences of what has been said in the meeting; denial of the worth of the meeting; a desire to escape from the group

Positive: Increased awareness of self or others; satisfaction from having gained recognition or acceptance; a sense of fulfillment from having contributed or received; motivation to begin planning for the future

Groups commonly want to continue the communication of the group meeting by carrying on informal discussions of problems beyond the meeting. If, however, the group assembles to work on problems, the expectation is that a staff member usually will be present. The group does

*The human brain tends to work so as to close off tasks rather than to leave issues incomplete or unresolved. One of the first researchers to note this was Zeigarnik [2] who found that subjects had better recall of interrupted tasks than of completed tasks. This phenomenon came to be known as the "Zeigarnik effect." In a sense, this effect is what the group leader creates: he poses an unresolved problem, which creates a tendency for the group members to continue being aware of the "incomplete task." The hope is that they will work for a solution.

†The foregoing discussion of summarizing group meetings includes material provided by James Uden.

not have the right to exclude staff with a comment such as "We group members are going to meet privately and work this thing out." If the issue must be private and confidential, then the students should wait for the next regular group meeting.

Sometimes as problems arise, members will want to call a special meeting of the group. Since formal group sessions already occupy several hours weekly, further proliferation of meetings is not encouraged; the group that continually holds extra meetings soon will have little to contribute in regular meetings. Intensive examination of problems should be reserved for the structured group meeting. A person can receive first aid at any time or place, but complicated treatment requires a properly controlled environment.

Occasionally, a group may try to keep things stirred up in order to avoid study or work. The constant disruption of school or work projects because of long, involved sessions is valueless. If the young people persist in spending large amounts of time in the discussion of problems when other activities are scheduled, deterrents may be necessary. Thus, if students spend an entire class period talking about a problem, staff may arrange for them to complete the work they missed at a later time (after school hours). However, the group should never be criticized for spending time in helping.

Another complication that arises from discussions outside the meeting is one of confidentiality—a particularly sensitive issue if charges and counter-charges are exchanged. A certain amount of confrontation may be necessary to allow members to correct one another or to clearly mark the problem; still, groups should not be engaged in continuous verbal explosions outside the meeting. The group session provides the appropriate climate where feelings can be safely expressed and evaluated.

A common question in starting a PPC program is the advisability of private individual communications with students. Certainly no rule obviates staff–student discussions, but sometimes a youth seeks out an adult in order to avoid communicating with his group. The youth may be very clever at playing the adult against the group: "I trust you, but I don't trust the group; can I talk with you about my problems?" Staff may respond with a statement such as "I'm sure that you care enough to help build your group so that members will trust one another; then you will feel free to share problems with the group."

NOTES

[1] Sir Arthur Conan Doyle, *The Sign of Four* (1890) in the collection of *Conan Doyle's Best Books,* (New York: P. F. Collier).
[2] B. Zeigarnik, "Das Behalten erledigter und underledigter Handlungen," *Psychologische Forschung* 9 (1927).

9

Cultivating
a Caring Culture

> Gardens are not made by singing: "Oh, how beautiful" and sitting in the shade.
>
> —Rudyard Kipling

NEUTRALIZING NEGATIVE PEER INFLUENCE

Since a positive culture cannot flourish in an atmosphere of chaos, an initial step in solving problems is to bring behavior within reasonable limits. In beginning PPC, staff do not suddenly give up control or abolish rules and regulations. Instead, established measures of discipline should continue until the students are able to assume responsibility for all behavior. As a positive group emerges, previous control measures can be gradually supplanted. Although intensive problem solving occurs in the group meeting, youth must assume the responsibility for managing problems whenever and wherever they arise. PPC groups exercise this responsibility in two main ways:

1. *Checking:* As a student begins to show a problem, the group gives him a cue or reminder to control himself. For example, if a person becomes angry and it appears that he may lose his temper, the group simply says to him, "Check yourself." This provides instant feedback on the unacceptability of the behavior and calls on the youth to control himself. In situations when verbal checking is inappropriate, students can give nonverbal cues to one another.

2. *Confronting:* In confronting, the group members show their concern by challenging negative, irresponsible behavior and making the student aware of the effect of his actions on others. Confronting is necessary if the student fails to respond to being checked or if the problem is serious enough to be marked clearly for later group discussion.

Peer pressure has no place in a PPC program unless it is an integral part of peer concern. A frequently asked question is whether group confrontation is not really a kind of punishment. While it certainly is not pleasant to be confronted by one's peers, the intent of such confrontation is not to punish but, rather, to help. Going to the dentist may hurt, but few would interpret the visit as punishment. The group is not trying to cause pain but to help the person change, and change is sometimes painful.

Some group programs are criticized because they permit young people to engage in what may best be termed *hazing*. Such activity is not tolerated in a positive peer culture. For example, in one group therapy program, a youth was expected to kneel in the center of the group throughout the entire group meeting. In another instance, the person who was the focus of the meeting was required to hang a toilet seat around his neck on which was painted the inscription, "I am crapping on people with my behavior." Whether dramatic or subtle, all negative peer pressure is totally unacceptable.

The group should not be allowed to do negative things to a member and then say to him, "We were just testing you to see how you would react." If any testing is to be done, it should be by staff, not students. Further, the group should not decide to punish itself. For example, a group may decide that because members have been irresponsible, no one should watch television for a week or everyone should run laps around the gymnasium. Staff may initially think self-applied consequences are good, but in reality the group is using simplistic means of suppressing the problem rather than resolving it.

The group is given permission to help but never to restrict or punish; neither should a group recommend to staff that restrictions be applied. Instead, the group works to eliminate the need of limits set by staff. If the group cannot handle a problem appropriately, then staff are responsible for moving in and settling limits.

Reclaiming the Negative Leader

Building a caring group culture requires that youth with leadership potential become involved in positive roles. In many groups, the youth with the most power wields a generally negative influence on his peers; so we should consider the identification and redirection of these negative peer leaders.

The *negative indigenous leader* (NIL) often is a youth for whom delinquency has become a way of life. He may be involved in numerous negative and illegal activities and is perhaps seldom apprehended. Usually NIL has considerable ability to con and to manipulate and views himself as slick and sly. In his home situation, he is able to control his parents or at least to avoid their control. He is highly status conscious and is successful at climbing to a position of power among his peers. He usually has average or above-average intelligence that may not be shown in testing, and he may be seriously underachieving in school. Even though he may not be physically strong, he carries himself in a confident manner and has the capacity to enlist others if force is required. When his status is threatened, he typically reasserts authority by setting up a confrontation with staff.

Usually NIL operates with assistants, here referred to as *lieutenants*. The lieutenants generally sit on either side of him in group meetings and stick close to him outside meetings. Staff may not even be aware of who the negative leader and his lieutenants are, but the group will usually be quite aware. The negative lieutenants are likely to be more obvious and accessible than the leader; so by noting who the negative students approach for advice, look to for approval, or seek to impress, one can often infer who the real leader is. This youth is quite adept at using the lieutenants to do his bidding, which may include scapegoating other members or the leader. The group as a whole is usually reluctant to bring up his problems, often out of fear of reprisal. When NIL does enter the group discussion, his questions usually command the group's attention, and he is able to redirect the group in whatever direction he wants.

The NIL usually cases the situation, plans his moves in advance, and keeps cool under stress. Since he is adept at playing roles, he assumes others are playacting, too. Sometimes NIL may present himself in a superficially positive manner when adults are around. NIL may overdo his positive performance for staff, and one can usually detect a note of insincerity in his put-on behavior. The NIL is adept at handling staff and often can succeed at boxing them into a corner and making them feel highly defensive.

PPC has developed a series of procedures for reclaiming NILs by transforming their influence into positive channels. In general, the NIL is not attacked directly; rather, his foundations of support are undercut. If one were to directly and publicly attack NIL, his lieutenants would rally the group to his cause, and the adult might find he was facing a unified negative gang. Therefore, the desired strategy is to capture the lieutenants.

Operating outside group meetings, staff begin to place pressure on the lieutenants. In ordinary circumstances, NIL would then come to their support, but he is blocked because demands on the lieutenants are so placed that they are isolated from his support.

1. *Holding the lieutenants responsible:* An attempt is made to place the lieutenants in a bind by making them responsible not only for their own behavior but also for that of NIL. Staff confront them, saying the lieutenants

do not really care for NIL, for if they did they would want to help him. Since the lieutenants are being accused of a lack of loyalty to NIL they are confused, and NIL is temporarily disoriented as well. Staff must continue to place pressure on lieutenants, make high demands, and point out that any problems NIL shows are their responsibility.

2. *Neutralizing the negative leader:* As staff maintain the initiative, the lieutenants find it increasingly difficult to continue their former relationships with NIL. As NIL sees his lieutenants becoming confused, he fears loss of support. He may become angry, blaming staff, lieutenants, the program, anybody but himself. At this point, he may engage in threatening behavior, may act out, or may try to regroup his forces. Forcing him into the open only gives the staff more instances of problem behavior that can be held up to the lieutenants as their responsibility. Now the smooth, well-oiled leadership machine is disrupted, and NIL has been neutralized.

3. *Providing a new role:* Since the intent is not to destroy NIL's influence but to redirect it, staff now begin to search for opportunities to reinvolve him in a positive way. Sometimes a crisis in the group can serve this purpose. Once the youth begins to assume a positive role, it is harder for him to turn around again and resume negative leadership. The youth has shown he is capable of helping, whatever his motives. Staff now begin to place expectations on him and do not allow him to extricate himself from this role. Pressure on NIL will have to continue only until the new role becomes established and self-rewarding.

The strong negative youth is very difficult to manage, and success depends on the mobilization of considerable resources. If the group cannot handle the student, then adults, individually or collectively, become responsible for managing him. On occasion NIL must be directly confronted with his behavior, usually in a one-to-one situation rather than in front of a group where he has an audience. Since the NIL is not easily confronted, staff may have to deal with him in special ways. Some possibilities are the following.

1. Have two staff members talk jointly with him and thus force him to respond to more than one individual confrontation about his behavior.
2. Have several staff briefly confront him in the course of a short period of time so that he loses confidence in knowing what might be coming next.
3. Make a list of incidents to use in confronting him about his behavior. The list has an ominous quality and allows the staff to maintain the initiative even if the youth can deny individual items on it.
4. Let him know that some influential outside figure (e.g., probation officer, girl friend) is coming in to talk with staff about how he is doing.

5. Communicate to the student that he is going to be treated as a person without influence or importance to the group because he uses his power only to hurt his followers.

Sometimes a strong negative student couches his resistance and rebellion in the form of political or racial militancy. Staff generally should not deal directly with the ideological issues involved because they would be engaging the individual on his own territory. Instead, staff should shift the focus to positive values, stating again and again in words and actions that people cannot hurt one another and that anyone who hurts others has a problem. Staff members must be united in the rejection of hurting behavior so that the youth is placed in an untenable position if he is really interested in hurting others but is camouflaging negative behavior by invoking some just cause. Of course, if the student's ideological commitment is sincere and is not based on destructive notions, no reason for conflict should exist. In any event, staff should never become defensive about the basic value of caring.

In effect, PPC always views the difficult youth as an asset, never as a liability. All the procedures for managing the difficult student have only one intent: The youth must abandon his negative, hurting leadership and begin to help members of his group and himself.

Managing Other Group Problems

The immature youth. This youth presents a set of challenges unlike those of the sophisticated negative youth. Less adequate students are easily led either toward delinquency or toward positive behavior, depending on circumstances. Usually they have very poor self-concepts with accompanying strong needs for approval from peers and adults alike. A group composed of immature youth may be quite sensitive to feelings but usually not aggressive enough to face difficult challenges. These students are apt to be emotionally erratic—highly motivated one minute and completely demoralized the next.

With immature youth, staff must continuously pair demands with support. Workers have found it helpful to alternate criticism with compliment, almost sentence for sentence. This technique is referred to as "punch and burp." For example, the adult may say, "That was childish behavior [criticism]. You are much more mature than that [compliment]." Such interactions are designed to strengthen the youth's self-concept while confronting his behavior.

Immature youth are in many ways more difficult to treat than are rebellious ones. They may respond more openly to adults, but their willingness to submit to authority may reflect an absence of self-direction. Staff who work with such youth must help them to learn to succeed without always depending on adults. The adult must be secure, relaxed, and warm, and he must set high expectations, encouraging the group to learn to handle things themselves. Still staff must be prepared to carry more responsibility with immature youth than with sophisticated delinquents.

The isolate. Operating on the fringes of the group, this youth can seldom make a full contribution to others or derive full benefits from group participation. While every person needs some time alone, and certainly no rule forbids periods of solitude, the group should always take note of instances of a member's isolative behavior. The reasons for a youth's separation from the mainstream of the group are numerous: (1) Pursuing a legitimate private interest or activity; (2) feeling ignored or ostracized by peers; (3) seeking to withdraw into a world of fantasy; (4) feeling sorry for self or seeking attention by sulking; (5) trying to "play it cool" and avoid confrontations; (6) having a life-style as a loner, a self-oriented person; (7) having little in common with other members of the group. Whatever the reason for isolation, the group needs to understand why a member is alone and help him to see that he can help himself and others only as he participates in the total life of the group.

The scapegoat. The scapegoat is a frequent management problem in group settings. Some believe it inevitable that every group will have a scapegoat. Certainly, most groups do have some status differentiation among their members, but in a true positive culture, status comes from helping one's peers. Stratification based on degrees of helpfulness is incompatible with the scapegoating process. The group must learn to refrain from attacking a person just because he is not liked, and the scapegoat must learn how his behavior causes others to treat him negatively.

The scapegoat is not always a weak individual but may be a person of whom others are afraid. Then the members may scapegoat by speaking disparagingly about the person behind his back. Such clandestine attacks on an individual are unacceptable in a positive culture. Groups should come to embrace the norm that "We don't talk about others when they aren't here to benefit from our observations." Sometimes a group decides to ignore a youth whom they would otherwise scapegoat, but this silent treatment may be only another kind of subtle rejection. Ostracism by one's peers is among the most severe forms of punishment, and a group has no more right to be indifferent to a troubled person than to attack him directly.

The physically abusive youth. This youth presents a particular challenge to both staff and group members. If a group is afraid to confront such a student, then staff confrontation may be necessary. The group should not feel that any member is so strong and dangerous that all the staff are afraid to deal with him. Rather, the group needs the security of knowing that in one way or another someone is able to manage any situation. Adults cannot be frightened of youth and still be effective. If a staff member finds that he is continually frightened, he should be transferred to a different type of student or should stop working with young people.

If a fight occurs between students in a group, other group members are responsible for stopping it. If they do not act, staff should quickly intervene and confront the nonfighting members with their responsibility to stop the hurting without hesitation. Of course, if the group cannot or will not intervene, staff must stop the fight, but only because the group failed to exercise this responsibility.

If one student is so upset and emotionally out of control that he could hurt himself or others, he may require temporary physical restraint. Staff can point out this need to students by asking, "Can't you see he needs your help?" Staff must be extremely observant of any such situations since in no way should physical restraint justify any aggressive, hurting behavior by those who are supposedly helping the individual.

If a student continues to intimidate others physically, staff may have to counter his indifference by quite intensely expressing concern. In a private conference, staff can pour out a series of demands and communicate with strong feeling that the youth will not be allowed to hurt those who are trying to help him. Staff should not get into an argument or even a discussion on this point, since it is a nonnegotiable demand: "You have no right to threaten or attack or hurt other people!" Certain staff members are more effective than others in setting these limits, but every setting should contain one or more persons who can fulfill this role. When the students learn that staff are not afraid to place demands on a hostile student, they as a group will feel more confident in dealing with the person.

The manipulative youth. To win some special favors, this youth often tries to butter up staff. Sometimes manipulative students go to great lengths to try to impress others that they are changing. They flaunt positive verbalizations; they correct peers with loud confrontations; they vow to stop breaking rules and claim they have reformed. Beneath all this, they are concerned only with impressing others, perhaps in hope of getting out of the program. The general response of the staff should be to mark this behavior, perhaps with a question such as, "When is Sam going to start working for the group instead of for staff?"

The manipulative individual's behavior in front of staff may be quite different from his actions in the presence of his peers. Staff must be careful not to fall for this manipulation but, rather, see it for what it is—a problem. Since some of these young people are well practiced at fooling adults, they sometimes succeed in their deception. However, staff need not be threatened but can point out to the student that even if he were able to fool the adults, he cannot fool all the members of his group.

On occasion, an entire group tries to manipulate a situation, most commonly in new groups where youth test the limits until they learn how to work appropriately on problems. For example, one common difficulty in beginning groups is to arrange for one member to run away, which then supposedly justifies all the other members in chasing him. In reality what has happened is that the entire group has run away. Since this mass exodus is only another example of problem behavior, staff should respond by placing responsibility back on those young people who are more interested in playing games than in helping.

STRENGTHENING POSITIVE PEER INFLUENCE

Building Cohesive Groups

The members of a cohesive group are bound to one another with strong feelings of unity and mutual loyalty; the greater the cohesiveness, the more impact the group will have on its members. In order to foster cohesiveness, PPC programs are so designed that group members are together as much as possible.

Youth in PPC become fully invested in one another's lives. Continuous exposure helps members to increase their awareness of problem behavior and facilitates transfer of learning to situations outside the meeting. Such procedures are in marked contrast to some group therapy programs in which members are not permitted even to contact one another outside group meetings.

In community-based programs, total group contact usually is not feasible, but by careful planning the members can still have extensive exposure to one another at times other than group meetings. Many natural opportunities for association outside the group already exist. Even if school classes are departmentalized, rather than self-contained, it may be possible to schedule subgroups of three or more youth into many or all of the same classes.

In residential settings, it is possible to keep the group intact 24 hours a day. The group can live in the same cottage, study in the same classroom, and work and play as a group. If members must be separated for some reason, the usual procedure is to keep at least three youth together, thus maintaining a viable subgroup of the larger group. While both staff and students may initially think the members will tire of such continual exposure, the real effect is just the opposite: Youth will come to prefer association with this group of persons whom they know and trust.

The common practice of housing two groups in the same cottage creates no particular problems so long as the groups hold separate meetings. In fact, the complexity that results when two groups must share the same building has some value. If conflicts arise between members of different groups, each group is responsible for dealing with its own members, but group territoriality should never become more important than helping, and if one group is unable to handle a serious problem, then members from another group may be asked to help. Such aid is an exception to the general guideline that groups should handle their own problems, and it should be monitored very carefully. The less effective group must not feel put down by the assistance it receives; the field of helping has little room for *competition* but much room for *cooperation*.

Sometimes groups display high levels of individual territoriality and strong antigroup feelings. Thus, a group member may say, "This is my room and my personal property; I want everybody else to keep out." Staff will need to counter this attitude. While an individual's right to both privacy and personal possessions cannot be denied, the predominant spirit should be one of shared openness rather than of selfish overpossessiveness.

Staff should try to diminish status consciousness in the group; therefore, to refer to a specific youth as "leader" of the group thereby supporting him in his quest for power, is never a good idea. Even if the student is positive, being so designated gives one individual too much power, and groups become overly dependent on such a student. In PPC, the only sign of status should be, "Who is the most helpful to others?"

Staff should not foster rivalries by playing different members against one another (e.g., "Nancy is new but already she is doing better than Amy"). Such comments do not build cohesiveness but only alienate group members. Some group programs fail because staff encourage formal or informal one-to-one relationships, such as buddy systems, which undercut group solidarity. If one group member is having problems, it might seem logical to assign another member to watch him. However, too often this becomes a babysitting operation and allows the rest of the group to abdicate responsibility for the youth. Staff must work constantly to hold the total group responsible for all of its members.

PPC programs try to establish a strong *esprit de corps* within the group. In countless different ways, staff strive to motivate youth by showing them they can do well and by reinforcing their positive feelings about themselves. Students never should be told that their group is no good; such statements will not motivate the members but will only lower group morale. The youth should believe that, based on their ability to help one another, they have "a great group."

One of the best ways of building cohesiveness is to provide opportunities for the group to succeed. For example, a group was mobilized to help search for a lost child in a heavily wooded area. When the youngster was found, the group members shared deep feelings of satisfaction and accomplishment, and group morale improved dramatically.

Staff should be continually alert for opportunities to place greater responsibilities on the group. In general, the more responsibility groups can assume, the stronger they will become. Thus, in some residential programs, groups are made responsible for doing their own cooking on weekends, cleaning their own quarters, painting the classrooms and facilities they use, and tutoring one another. Delegation of responsibility may require a shift in staff expectations: instead of saying "They couldn't do that," adults must learn to ask "Why couldn't they do that?"

In settings with several groups, it is useful at intervals to bring all the groups together to meet with the program director. In these meetings, the groups can be given feedback, can receive recognition for doing a good job, and can be directed toward further challenges. Sometimes group cohesiveness can be strengthened through more specific procedures. For example, many PPC programs periodically obtain large photographs of the group and post them in conspicuous places. However, no morale-building techniques can foster a positive group without the support of adults who believe in the great potential of young people.

When a group is doing well, it may be helpful to give them credit by taking the entire group to a conference of teachers or social workers where they can explain their positive peer culture. Even if the professional audience is initially a bit skeptical, a strong positive group can handle the situation, and the recognition will be a gratifying experience for the students.

One of the best indicators of group solidarity is that the members gravitate to one another and operate as a unit rather than as individuals. In many youth settings whenever 8 or 10 young people are mingling together, staff become anxious that a gang or mob is developing, but when a positive culture is established, this unity will be a sign of a strong, cohesive group.

The Creative Use of Stress

In certain circumstances, it is possible to improve group performance by placing more stress on the group. It cannot be too strongly emphasized that any use of stress must be carefully planned and implemented; the intention is to motivate students toward change rather than to create negativism or excessive anxiety. All staff should be aware of the purpose and procedure to be used in applying stress to a group or individual. The decision to use stress must take these factors into consideration: (1) the specific objectives one is trying to achieve; (2) the ability of staff to employ stress appropriately; (3) the group's capacity for handling stress positively; (4) the individual's capacity for handling stress positively; (5) any ethical considerations raised by the interventions. Because of such complexities, it is never the prerogative of students in a PPC group to purposefully create stressful situations for their peers. Thus, the group members' attempt to provoke a negative peer "to make him mad so he'll talk" would be interpreted as causing a problem rather than helping to solve a problem.

In using stress, any implication of punishment must be completely avoided. An example of stress without punishment will serve to clarify this concept.

> Without announcing plans ahead of time, staff arranged to take on a camping trip a group that was totally unable to function as a cohesive unit. In ordinary circumstances these youth would have been restricted from camping because they were not behaving properly. Staff accompanied the group to a wilderness area where the members had to work cooperatively in order to obtain shelter

and sustenance. The outing achieved the intended effect, because the students began to assume much more responsibility and to work together in a cooperative manner.

If a group is in a state of tranquil indifference and nobody wants to bother with working on problems, then staff may need to disrupt the status quo. For example, in residential schools when a group has become stagnant and overly satisfied, the rotation of living arrangements so as to create sufficient disruption to social patterns has helped at times to move the group toward renewed vitality.

If the group is unconcerned about a serious problem, then staff may have to design a response that will awaken the students to the gravity of the situation. For example, two boys stole a car and had an accident. Because they were treating the whole escapade as a lark, the problem was escalated in a dramatic manner. Staff called in the owner of the car (to work out his reimbursement) and involved the families of both boys as well as their girl friends. The girls were told in the boys' presence that although it might be easy to find new boyfriends who didn't have to steal, they probably wanted to help the boys solve the problems that kept getting them into trouble.

In extreme situations, restrictions can be applied to raise concern in the group. Two girls in a group home showed numerous problems, but the other members were completely insensitive to the matter. After the girls had been apprehended while shoplifting for the third time in as many weeks, the rest of the group was placed on restriction, without explanation. The group was left to figure out that they were responsible for helping these girls but had not fulfilled their responsibility. In any use of restriction, the intent must never be to punish individuals or the group for misbehavior. Rather, even in these exceptional cases, the goal is to confront the group, in a forceful manner if necessary, with the reality of their irresponsibility.

Fostering Productivity

Contemporary society does not always expect young people to be productive but in fact places them in noncontributory, parasitic roles. Many current laws even keep young people from entering the job market, supposedly to protect them from exploitation. Instead of developing self-concepts based on feelings of accomplishment, youth view themselves as burdens on others or perhaps may even feel that the world is obliged to provide for them. Youth have abundant opportunities to be consumers, but they are not always given the chance to be productive. The distinction between production and consumption is as basic as in the distinction between giving and receiving.

PPC assumes that involvement in productive and creative activities is of greater value than is passive consumption. Many existing youth programs really are little more than futile attempts to provide entertainment and possibly keep youth out of trouble, but such entertainment fails to meet the real needs of young people. They might better be participants than spectators, play musical instruments than listen to music, or rebuild junk cars than aimlessly ride the streets. This active philosophy may well go against the mainstream of thought in a society where the average television set is operating several hours a day.

Educators have long been aware that it is better to be an active than a passive learner. Yet the only active person in many classrooms is the teacher, except perhaps for students who display behavior problems. Schools all too often expect students to sit quietly and passively as knowledge is fed into them. One way that a PPC program achieves active learning is by involving students in teaching one another. Almost every student has some skill or knowledge that one of his peers has not yet mastered. The person who teaches derives as much benefit as the person being taught, as any teacher who has worked to keep ahead of a class can readily attest.

A wide variety of work activities should be incorporated into PPC programs. Work should not be used to punish youth who show problems, because such a use communicates to students that work is not a positive activity but is drudgery. Instead, all activities should be meaningful and should give students a chance to get to know themselves within a real-life situation. The group members may initially have great difficulty in working together in an efficient and cooperative manner, and they may resist any expectations that they produce work. Staff should not try to make all work "easy" or "fun," since youth need to learn that work, even though meaningful, will not always be enjoyable. Further, youth should not expect to be paid for everything they do. With these strong expectations about work, almost inevitably certain youth will balk at helping their group when work projects are scheduled. Refusal should not be surprising during the initial stages of group development, and staff should use the issue in developing team spirit among group members. Realistic problems that arise from work projects should be discussed in group meetings.

Staff must take an aggressive role in fostering productive programming. Properly operating PPC groups are not concerned merely with entertaining themselves but are able to produce an unusual amount of work, in the school setting and beyond it. PPC groups willingly volunteer their services to day care centers and homes for the aged, sweep sidewalks for the elderly, clean up roadways, work in recycling centers, and help to improve the environment. This important aspect of PPC is discussed more fully in the following section.

CURRICULUM FOR CARING

Student involvement in volunteer activities in the community, often referred to as *service-learning*, offers exciting opportunities for redirecting youth into positive, productive roles. While the contributions of well-adjusted "model" youth in community service are well recognized, we are only beginning to recognize that all young people need and can benefit from such service [1].

The foundation of PPC is to teach young people to help one another. Bringing a group to this point is a major achievement—but what then? How can we insure that helping behavior is genuine and that it will transfer outside the peer group? Unless caring values and behavior generalize beyond the PPC group, we only might have taught students how to play a ritualized conning game and created a "greenhouse effect" which is un-related to the real world. Admittedly, the aspirations of service-learning with troubled youth is ambitious. We are not content to merely *neutralize* negative peer influence; the goal is to *reverse* this behavior, making youth an asset to their communities.

If young people are to develop competence and self-esteem, they must experience opportunities to affect the world [9]. But while youth long for a feeling of importance, "the usual adult approach . . . is to build them a new playground or teen-town where they are told to 'go and play some more'" (Combs, cited by Hamacheck) [4].

Deprived of opportunities for productivity, shunted into consumptive roles, young people come to learn that their presence makes very little difference in the world. Rotter [6] developed the concept of *locus of control* which refers to the degree to which an individual assumes responsibility for the impact of one's own behavior. Many troubled youth believe that they have little real control over their lives. Their irresponsibility is closely related to their external locus of control (i.e., feelings of being helpless victims, fate, or the whims of powerful others). Involvement in successful experience in service-learning can challenge young people's assumptions that they are worthless and help them develop positive roles [8].

As youth transcend themselves, they become committed to persons or causes greater than their individual egos. Service-learning is an antidote to the narcissism, malaise, and antisocial life-styles so common in today's troubled youth. Among the benefits that can accrue from service-learning are these: (1) enhancing moral development toward the higher levels such as a respect for the dignity of all human beings; (2) causing others to treat youth as worthy members of the community; (3) providing ample opportunities to experience mature levels of caring; (4) offering the opportunity for exposure to positive role models; (5) reducing the discontinuity and polarization that exists between the two worlds of adults and children [7].

A wide range of service-learning projects have been highly successful with PPC groups. Some of these are of short duration, while others are carried on regularly over a period of many months, including: serving as teacher aides at a community day-care center, assisting in Special Olympic events for the handicapped, working with retarded children at a special school, earning money to provide food for a needy family, chopping firewood for the disabled, and visiting shut-in citizens. As Fantini [3] has stated, the range of possible service-oriented activities is virtually without limit if educators use a little thought and imagination.

Procedures for Service Learning

Since many youth initially disparage values of service, a formidable obstacle to successful service-learning is to design ways to motivate and involve students. Among the procedures that have been developed are these:

1. Make the project seem challenging to appeal to their strength (e.g., "this will be a tough job" rather than "this will be easy").
2. Stress what they can do for others to counter dependency and appeal to needs for autonomy. ("These people will need your help" rather than "This will help you not to feel sorry for yourself").
3. Seek a balance between varied short projects and the need for long-term commitment in ongoing helping relationships.
4. Make projects exciting, spontaneous rather than regimented. Some groups have even helped in disasters of floods or tornadoes or in searches for a lost child. A somewhat different example of a spontaneous project was seen in a group that successfuly solicited surplus flowers from a department store the day after Mother's Day in order that these might be redistributed to residents of a nursing home "who didn't have anybody give them flowers on Mother's Day."

Despite the great diversity of projects, most service-learning activities proceed through four stages, namely *identification, orientation, implementation,* and *evaluation.*

Identification of project. In this initial stage, staff work independently or with students to identify potential areas of service. The projects must meet several criteria: These must not be "make-work" but reflect a genuine need that exists in a community; care must be taken that students are not exploited through the particular voluntary work they are to undertake; the task must be appropriate to the maturity and sophistication of the young people involved. One demanding project involved a group of delinquents in a group home who reached a level of maturity that they could successfully work with younger predelinquents in a neighborhood recreation program. An example of a project geared to a group of less mature younger students was the preparation of a home and yard for a new refugee family, planting flowers and bringing toys to the children. Staff must determine that the project is in fact feasible, that the logistics of money, regulations, travel, etc., will be workable and will not interfere with the successful consummation of the project.

Orientation of students. The next stage is to orient the students to the proposed project and to determine their possible interest in service. This involves exposing young people to concepts, people, or situations so that they develop an awareness of the existence of a need for service. In some cases, the need may be dramatically self-evident. In the case of a tornado, one had only to explain to the group that an entire community had been devastated and volunteers were sought to help clear the rubble. In another situation, the need may be introduced more obliquely to arouse interest. A psychologist from a state hospital for retarded children came to present a color slide show on mental retardation. This created initial interest that was followed by a tour of the hospital. Only at that point, dependent upon the reaction of young people during this period of orientation, was a decision made that a specific proposal for involving the youth as recreation aides might be placed before the students. When students are aware of a need and motivated to be of service, then staff and youth can begin planning the third stage—participation in service activity.

Implementation. Young people are involved to the maximum extent possible in organizing the project, executing the activity, and evaluating the service experience. As seen from the great variety of activities, each project requires its own unique pattern for organization and implementation. Successful involvement in providing a genuine service to others usually increases motivation for further service. The project can continue until the need is met and/or until new challenges are desired. At that point, students and staff are again ready to identify further potential areas of service.

Evaluation. Almost all evaluations of projects to date are based on ongoing, informal, interpersonal feedback among staff, students, and those being served. In the final analysis, the goal is to create a positive caring atmosphere where service to others becomes a life-style; youth should not experience such activity as some kind of "treatment program" but as a community of humans reaching out to one another. While qualitative evaluation is useful, nevertheless, there is a need to develop creative evaluative designs to more precisely assess the nature of the impact of service-learning on students and those they serve.

Sometimes a project will not fully succeed in reaching its desired objective. The common reasons for failure of service-learning are the following:

1. *Inadequate planning.* Sometimes the logistics are more overpowering than the motivation to help. When, where, what tools are needed, what transportation, who supervises, etc. All require consideration.
2. *Overly complex task.* A sophisticated group can execute a complex task. For example, one delinquent group built a picnic pavilion at the Campfire Girls campground. Not all groups would have skills for this.
3. *Overly complex human relationships.* Sometimes a group of immature youth may need to begin with a motor test (e.g., cleaning up a park) before they are ready to deal with a more interpersonal project (e.g., visiting senior citizens).

4. *Adult imposed projects.* Unless youth feel involved in the planning, they may not feel ownership. If projects are "theirs," they will work much harder.
5. *Institutionalized helping.* As with any other activity, one can get into a rut. Like a good game, one should quit while the activity is still enjoyable.

Perhaps the most common difficulty is that most of a group want to help, but an isolated individual resists. The usual approach in these cases is to involve youth in trying to understand why the reluctant person is holding back. Their creativeness in dealing with this can truly be impressive.

> A 17-year-old unmarried student whose girlfriend was about to deliver their child was generally reluctant to participate in any helping projects. Rather than to continue trying to convince this youth that he should care more about others, the group members adopted the strategy of initiating a car wash with all of the proceeds being given for the support of his soon-to-be-born illegitimate child. This young man was noticeably moved by this expression of concern from his peers and he became a fully contributing member of the group.

An important area of need is to develop more effective means of continuing to provide rules for helping after the student leaves the group program. This is a crucial need with the student leaving a treatment program returning to a community setting. It is essential to communicate with the school personnel and others concerning the changes that have occurred in a young person and give examples of specific projects in which he has been involved. Once they understand the concept, many counselors and principals are willing to seek creative ways to use the students' resources in the school setting.

The systematic utilization of service-learning can make a decided contribution toward transforming youth who are viewed as societal liabilities into valuable assets. However, as Saurman and Nash [7] caution, preoccupation with the personal development of youth must not be allowed to obscure the basic purpose of service to others, lest this become yet another kind of narcissism, however self-fulfilling. Keith-Lucas [5] has suggested that while positive growth is an outcome of service, the overriding goal should always be the self-actualization of those being served, not of those doing the service. Otherwise, concludes Buber [2], those who enter into helping with the expectation of satisfying their own needs are condemned to a relationship that will never be complete.

NOTES

[1] L. Brendtro and A. Nicholaou, "Hooked on Helping," *Synergist* 10, no. 3: 38–41.
[2] M. Buber, *I and Thou* (New York: Charles Scribner and Sons, 1970).
[3] M. Fantini, "Disciplined Caring," *Phi Delta Kappan* 62 (1980): 182–184.

[4] D. Hamachek, *The Self in Growth, Teaching and Learning* (Englewood Cliffs, N.J.: Prentice-Hall, 1965).

[5] A. Keith-Lucas, *Foundations and the Needs of the Nation,* Report of the Committee for the Study of National Service (Washington, D.C., 1979).

[6] J. Rotter, "Generalized Expectancies for Internal versus External Control of Reinforcement, *Psychological Monographs* 80, no. 1, whole no. 609 (1966): 1–28.

[7] K. Saurman and R. Nash, "An Antidote to Narcissism," *Synergist* 9, no. 1 (1980): 15–18.

[8] S. Thompson, "A Chance to Change," *Synergist* 9, no. 2 (1980): 2–5.

[9] R. White, "The Urge towards Competence," *American Journal of Occupational Therapy* 25, no. 6 (1971): 271–274.

10

Organization in
Residential Settings

> The committee propose that an old ship be obtained
> and fitted up for the accommodation of 150 boys.
> —Massachusetts Board of Charities (1865)

ROADBLOCKS TO TREATMENT

After more than a century of searching for better approaches, too few
child-caring institutions really achieve their stated aims of developing,
correcting, or rehabilitating youth. Despite numerous attempts to channel
more money and energy into improving programs, failure seems the rule
rather than the exception. Although public concern with inadequate institutions is not new, the problems have persisted.*

> In a study of the history of a large children's institution it was shown that an
> ineffective and destructive program had continued over a period of 100 years. In
> regular manner, approximately once every decade, the undesirable conditions
> were brought to light by some exposé in the press. This was regularly followed
> with a flurry of administrative activity and some sort of reorganization. Then the
> institution would settle back for a few more years until someone again would
> bring the substandard conditions to the public eye.†

*The status of children's institutions was critically reviewed by Pappenfort,
Kilpatrick, and Roberts [4]. For an excellent research analysis of the organization of
institutions for delinquents see Street, Vinter, and Perrow [6].
†Unpublished paper by Hermann Saettler, University of Illinois Department of
Special Education, 1967.

Because of such experiences, some have come to view all institutional programs as ineffective, and any residential placement as undesirable. Here, we consider some of the inefficiencies frequently found in residential programs. Only as such difficulties are resolved will an institution be able to provide an effective treatment program.

The Wrong Youth

Many institutions are serving a large number of young people who do not belong in residence. Some have come into the setting because of short-comings in the legal, judicial, or correctional process or because of the unavailability of appropriate resources. Handling many of these youth in community programs might be better than removing them from their natural environments.*

Some programs have considerable control over intake, particularly in private child-care facilities, which often limit admission to those who do not present severe management problems. While a benign population con-tributes to the peace, tranquility, and stability of the residential setting, such programs are not responsive to the needs of society's most troubled youth.

Political or financial factors pressure some institutions to utilize all available bed space, which actually is inefficient, since decisions on intake may reflect the excess availability of space rather than a youngster's real needs for the program. Sometimes with declining population, an institution will admit students who will not be likely to succeed in the program but who, for a short period of time, will ease the "problem" of a partially empty facility.

Improper Length of Care

The duration of care frequently is determined by factors unrelated to treatment progress. Many institutions require that a youth remain in the program a specified period of time, and the minimum lengths of stay are very arbitrary and may be unrelated to individual needs. Clearly, it would be more efficient to release a youngster from the program as soon as he is able to function in the community, but it is equally unwise to place a youngster in a program for a very brief period of time if a longer stay is needed to effect changes. Too many institutions release youth when they show conforming behavior; too few determine the length of stay solely on the basis of clear treatment goals for each youngster.

*For a classic research experiment on the question of which types of youth are best treated only in the community and which need residential care as the treatment of choice, the reader is referred to Palmer [3].

Isolated Professionals

If one were compelled to identify which staff members in an institution were most dispensable, at least temporarily, one might select those with the highest status—the professionals. In most residential settings, power is in the hands of the professional staff, and frontline workers are not accorded professional status even though they are directly involved in the treatment process. Sometimes the professional designs his own job responsibilities around what he has been trained to do or likes to do rather than what really needs to be done; so, despite the proliferation of professional services, the program may still be ineffective.

Administrators seldom question the practice of using professionals to supervise other staff in jobs that the professionals themselves can not perform. Frequently, the professional not only has little to offer those who must work on the front line but also is able to insulate himself from the strains and pressures of the day-by-day operation, thus minimizing his contribution to the program. Perhaps the most glaring symbol of professional inefficiency is the private office. The person who sits isolated in a comfortable, carpeted office can never become involved in the dynamic, on-going life of the institution. Only with full participation can the professional make a full contribution.

Complications in Communication

The number of different staff who work in an institution make imperative the considerable time spent in communication. Departmental meetings, clinical meetings, sectional meetings, cottage meetings, and in-service training meetings all consume large blocks of time that might better be spent in other ways. In one extremely "comprehensive" multidisciplinary treatment program, nearly 50% of certain staff's time is spent in meetings. Apparently, what one is paying for in placing a youngster in such an institution is time for the staff to communicate with one another about what they are doing.

Despite repeated attempts at communication, the net result frequently is that staff members cancel one another's efforts. What the therapist does in his office is sometimes undone by the child-care worker. The recreation worker may feel at cross purposes with the work supervisor. The teacher's efforts may be canceled by the social service staff. So it goes, as large numbers of individuals attempt to "do their thing." Somehow we hope that the youth will benefit amidst all these pressures, conflicts, and inconsistencies.

Cafeteria Approaches

In an attempt to develop a workable program, many institutions draw ideas from several divergent approaches. All too often the setting that tries to be all things to all people succeeds at practically nothing, and the danger exists regardless of the program's theoretical orientation. For example, an attempt to mix behavior modification techniques or psychoanalytic therapy with PPC would result in an adulteration of each of the separate orientations. Standing alone, each approach may be clear and systematic, but the eclectic mixture usually lacks any semblance of logical consistency. Frequently, the separate approaches prescribe different responses to a given problem, which inevitably leads to considerable staff confusion about what exactly is expected.

Parkinson's Law

Parkinson's law holds that work expands so as to fill the time available for its completion. Therefore, an organization will, over a period of time, appear to require more employees. This principle certainly applies to institutions for the care of children and youth, perhaps because of the almost universal tendency to see the cause of any problem as a shortage of personnel. The assumption is that if one were able to secure additional staff, the difficulty would disappear. Certainly, staff shortages are acute in some institutions, but in many more, human resources are abundant, even though employees may not realize it. One reason that workers commonly believe a staff shortage exists is because the program is not achieving the stated goals; staff call for additional help in the hope of relieving their frustrations.

Peer Culture Cancels Treatment Efforts

Perhaps the greatest inefficiency of all is the conflicting peer culture. The staff can be excellently trained, endowed with strong treatment motivation, superbly organized, well paid, and operating in a magnificent physical plant; nevertheless, the young residents have their own organization, which effectively resists many or all of the staff's treatment interventions. This inmate subculture has been well documented by research in prisons, mental hospitals, and youth institutions.* The peer subculture emerges as one of the most potent influences in every group setting for youth, and all too often it overpowers the treatment program. An institution that ignores the peer subculture, or only incidentally deals with it, is courting failure.

TEAMWORK PRIMACY

The management system of a human-service organization should be matched to the treatment methodology. Thus, while a centralized, authoritarian model would match a behavior modification program, PPC is

---

*For a classic study of this, see Goffman [2].

best matched to a participative management system (Babcock and Sorenson [1]). The core of such a model of participative management is a system for teamwork.

Staff teamwork should be the highest, single, administrative priority in a treatment institution. Many administrators strive to achieve teamwork, but few succeed in reaching their goals. PPC programs in residential settings operate within a specific organizational model designed to overcome the communication problems and intrastaff conflicts that characterize most institutions.

Known as "teamwork primacy," the model is a radical departure from traditional systems of organization and administration. This approach does not require additional staff members, since often they would be only part of the problem and not part of the solution. Likewise, teamwork primacy requires an absolute minimum of middle administrators, in contrast to the bureaucratic proliferation of staff roles in many institutions.

> A large, heavily funded, milieu treatment center operated with a ratio of three staff for every child in residence but still was unable to provide an effective program. Every time a new problem arose, the solution was to add another staff member. As the number of employees increased, so did communication problems and staff conflict, and the program simultaneously became more expensive and less effective. At this point someone suggested that a possible solution would be to involve staff in sensitivity groups so they could learn to get along more amicably. No one even thought of phasing out some positions in order to create a more efficient organization.

The implementation of PPC usually enables existing staff to handle problems with much less difficulty than before. Sometimes, after the positive culture has been established, employees themselves have suggested staff reductions. Many authorities on residential treatment feel that an ideal on-duty ratio of staff to students is one child care worker for every five youth, which is too many for a PPC program. A strong group culture cannot develop if so many adults are always around to cancel the young people's need to take responsibility. Adults need not be present in sufficient number to overpower young people; it is essential that the available adults function in a fully coordinated manner.

Just as PPC youth are formed into efficient and cohesive groups, so also must PPC staff be developed into efficient and cohesive teams. Generally, a team of no more than 10 staff members communicates and coordinates most effectively. A team of 25 staff members will not work well enough to make it worth the effort. Imagine a basketball, baseball, or football team with 25 persons on the playing field, trying to coordinate their activities!

A program organized around "departments" usually fails to achieve teamwork, since departmental loyalties create conflicts when staff must work closely together; hence departmental allegiance must be replaced with loyalty to the team. Likewise, true teamwork seldom is achieved if many hierarchal relationships exist within the team. Teamwork primacy invests both power and responsibility in all team members; therefore, no team member should be in an employer–employee or supervisory relationship with any others on the team. This structure is clearly in contrast with traditional notions of "teamwork" in which the supervisor conducts a meeting from the end of the table while all others listen politely, deferring to his greater authority and supposedly greater wisdom.

A Blueprint for Forming Staff Teams

Regardless of how large an institution may be, it must be reconceptualized as a number of smaller self-contained institutions, each no larger than one cottage. The cottage should contain one PPC (nine youth) or some multiple of one group; for example, an institution may have larger cottages that contain two groups of nine each. Individuals in the groups should stay together as close to 100% of the time as possible.

A cottage team is composed of all staff that have significant regular contact with the youth in the cottage—that is, every child-care, educational, and clinical staff member who works with the group. A half-dozen child-care staff may work in the cottage, and they would be on the team. The school program could be organized in a team-teaching format so that two teachers provide most of the educational experience for this group, and they would be on the team. Finally, the group leader responsible for both groups in the cottage would be on the team.

Every staff member's shift must be so arranged that he is available weekly for a team meeting of approximately 2 hours. If a staff member cannot be regularly available to meet with the team, he should not be allowed regular contact with the youth in the cottage. Students do not meet with the cottage teams, and the discussions are not communicated to the students but remain confidential within the staff community.

Everything important to the effective operation of the program is the province of the team. No topic of conversation is sacred, and the team meeting cannot be circumvented. Every responsibility that the team can possibly assume should be handled at that level. Thus, team meetings are used to develop clinical plans, evaluate the progress of students, resolve staff conflicts, schedule activities, and approve home visits or releases. The team does not have authority to expel students or to accept or reject applicants; these decisions are made at the administrative level, and the team is responsible for the treatment plan.

All members have equal opportunity for involvement and take turns in serving as monthly team chairman. If a staff member is unable to serve in rotation as chairman, he probably should not be leading young people. The team works from an agenda, and the chairman's only major responsibility is to see that the group efficiently uses the allotted meeting time adequately to cover agenda items.

Certain team members may be overly controlling or underinvolved, but the other members are responsible for achieving their full and balanced participation. If one person continually dominates the team, he is a liability and not an asset; if one team member fails to do his part, all others on the team are affected and are responsible for dealing with the failure. The most valuable and influential member of the team is the one who can develop the competence and strength of other members.

When the institution's administrator is concerned about an issue, he communicates directly with the cottage team, placing the responsibility on them as a group to deal with the matter. While teams are conducting their weekly meetings, the director rotates from one to another to monitor their functioning, to impart information, and to respond to the issues staff may raise. When he visits the meeting, the director does not preside over the team. Usually, he will not stay for the entire period, since his continued presence would undercut the team's need to operate with significant autonomy.

When the team feels that certain policy or administrative changes are in order, their recommendations for changes are made to the administrator, who then will either accept the recommendation or decline it with an explanation of his action. The administrator's role is to provide treatment direction as he delegates to the team responsibility for treatment decisions.

When all of the staff assigned to a group are meeting with the team, who is supervising the youth? Team meeting times usually are staggered to allow workers from different cottages to relieve one another for a couple of hours each week so that the entire staff can attend team meetings.

Some member of the team serves as secretary, recording the minutes of the meeting and making them available to members and administration. In addition, the team keeps a log of all pertinent notations necessary for clear communications between weekly meetings. Generally, this log "follows the group" as the students move from cottage to school or to other areas in the program.

As staff teams begin to assume responsibility for the total treatment program, true accountability develops. Workers begin to take a much greater interest in their particular group, and long-existing barriers to communication begin to crumble. As staff become more directly involved in the ongoing treatment program, a decided boost to morale is seen.

Although the implementation of teamwork primacy requires certain organizational rearrangements, marked improvement in staff coordination has resulted in every setting where this model has been employed. Teamwork primacy works as well in a large institution as in a small institution. The effect is to insulate a small group of staff and young people so that they can work together to develop an effective program.

TREATMENT ISSUES

Control versus Treatment

Our nation's most seriously aggressive youth are often found in residential treatment and correctional settings. Prior to the implementation of PPC in many of these centers, brutality and intimidation was a way of life. Students assaulted staff, staff assaulted students or controlled them with other highly coercive structures, and raw power ruled the institutional culture. Thus, it is not surprising that physical coercion has long been at the core of the control structure of many residential programs for difficult populations. In such institutions, detention rooms, quiet rooms, time-out rooms, isolation rooms, or lock-ups are widely used to deal with serious problem behavior. When PPC is being implemented in these settings, this control feature should not be eliminated immediately; to do so would only create unnecessary staff resistance. When the groups become positive, discontinuance or at least curtailment of physical confinement will be possible.

Temporary removal from the group may be necessary in extreme circumstances when a person is a serious danger to himself or others and so may need the control of secure confinement. All staff who work with the student should become involved in visiting the confined youth, reviewing with him what has happened, and communicating their concern. When possible, members of the group should visit the student; again, the emphasis must be on helping, and the group should not wield the power of deciding to "keep him locked up."

Confinement is not a punishment and never should be given for a defined time, or it will be viewed as a sentence. Typically, the group visits, a few members at a time, to assess the student's progress. After all the members have visited and the group feels they are able to deal with the student again, he should be released from the confined situation and reintegrated with the group. In no situation should the group be perceived as the agent that is keeping the student in confinement; staff must bear full responsibility for using such drastic measures.

When a student in a treatment setting is not able or willing to control himself, some system of management is necessary. In many cases, mature PPC groups under the close supervision of staff have been able to assist in temporarily supplying controls, even to the point of physical restraint if necessary. For example, a girl in a state training school physically attacked a teacher (who was much smaller than the student), and the group skillfully intervened and restrained the youth until she calmed down. Peer groups also regularly have taken appropriate action to stop fights that develop between two students. Nevertheless, such use of the group for physically restraining peers raises weighty issues.

Physical restraint by staff is employed in many treatment settings as a therapeutic alternative to locked physical isolation. Pfeiffer [5] notes that while few would question a responsible, trained adult exercising such control, the use of students has been controversial. In the days before peer group treatment, all forms of "barn bossing" and intimidation were called "peer pressure" ana many state child-welfare statutes expressly forbid delegating discipline to youth. The great concern with institutional child abuse in recent years has called into question presumably therapeutic restraint by peers (and sometimes even by adults). However, to totally forbid therapeutic restraint leads to undesirable alternatives: transferring control to guards or police-type personnel, inappropriate use of medications to chemically control youth, and relying on architectural restraints to lock up youth.

In summarizing his discussion of these issues, Pfeiffer [5] makes several recommendations:

1. Physical containment must be limited to only last resort, and if possible entirely eliminated through training of staff and group in non-physical forms of help and support.
2. Staff must guarantee that physical restraint only occurs in appropriate situations with trained staff supervising and bearing responsibility. Groups should not be given authority for restraint when staff are not physically present to facilitate, monitor, and report.
3. Supervisory and administrative staff must be aware of each physical containment and share in the responsibility of ensuring that no abusive elements are present.
4. Parents or guardians must be informed of every incident where physical restraint was used with such information as why restrained, by whom, for how long, and any complaints or injuries.

Since alternative systems of physical restraint (e.g., locked isolation) can have damaging, even lethal effects, there will probably continue to be a potentially positive role for human restraints in certain special situations. If physical restraint is to be a benign or therapeutic intervention, then it must be employed with extreme professional sensitivity and vigilance.

The Communication of Progress

A system for providing periodic progress reports has been developed for use in PPC programs when a court or social agency refers the student. Communication is in the form of a monthly progress letter made available to the group meeting and then sent to the referring agency. The letter is a description of the student's progress for that month and contains opinions from his staff and group.

The letter serves as a clear report to the referral agency about the progress of students in the program. Since youth frequently are quite concerned about how court or agency personnel view them, the letter also serves as a motivator. The letter is written in nontechnical language that all students and staff can understand. Further, the progress letter can serve to cue the group on staff expectations, thus improving communication with the students.

Typically, the first letter reports the negative behavior and attitudes that are causing problems. Ideally, the letters that follow the initial report show continual improvement as the student becomes a more positive and helpful member of the group. The final letter to the referral agency indicates the student's readiness to return to his home and community.

Although letters can be written in a variety of formats, many group leaders have found that a straightforward, one-page letter of five or six paragraphs is appropriate. The letter may include discussion of such topics as these:

1. *How the group leader sees the student:* A brief statement of the student's problems is presented, using the vernacular of the PPC Problem-Solving List. Other terminology not on the list may be used, provided it is concrete and easily understood. The group leader should avoid the tendency to make overly positive statements.

2. *How staff see the student:* Various staff members may perceive the student in different ways, and all these perspectives should be incorporated. Incidents may be given as evidence of problems, keeping phraseology simple and concise. A report of academic progress and performance in the work situation is included in this section.

3. *How the group sees the student:* Here one can cite the problems group members have identified, noting whether the student is seriously working on his problems and whether he is seen as helping other members of the group.

4. *How the student views self and group:* Here one can include information about the student's self-concept, his willingness to change, the degree to which he is trusting his group, and whether he views the group as helpful or as a threat.

5. *Community influences:* Included here are observations on how the student relates to family and peer group and how he responds to other community influences. Reference can be made in this section to placement plans for the student.

Certainly nothing is rigid in the preceding format and much more elaborate reporting may be required in many agencies. The overriding goal is the straightforward communication of progress. Although the letter will be sent to the agency worker who made the referral, it is often useful to send a copy to the judge, referee, or other person in authority, since the group members will thereby ascribe greater importance to the report. Generally, sending progress letters to parents seems to lower rather than increase the youth's motivation.

The letter should give a clear picture of the youth's progress in the program, but the contents never should violate specific confidences. If students get the feeling that sensitive topics discussed in the meeting will be reported to court personnel, the effect on open communication within the group will be disastrous.

The procedure for reading the letter in the group meeting is as follows:

1. The group leader always will have the progress letter available at the group meeting that falls closest to the monthly anniversary of the student's enrollment.

2. Before the session begins, the student whose 1-month anniversary letter is available should exercise the responsibility of asking the group leader to read his letter; then the leader will read it to the group.

3. If the student does not ask to have his letter read, the group leader will not force the letter on the group but in summary will point out that although a letter was available for reading, apparently the student did not want to have it read. This statement places on the student the responsibility for keeping track of when his progress letter is due and for asking to have it read if he is interested. In a properly functioning group, students rarely miss the opportunity of hearing their monthly reports.

4. After the letter is read, the students have a brief opportunity to respond. While the discussion of letters should not become long and involved since the meeting must get under way, the group should have an opportunity to respond to the letter. If the group makes some good suggestion after it hears the letter, the leader will want to incorporate the thought into the final progress letter mailed to the agency.

5. Progress letters should be directly available to all other members of the staff team, since they are not the private property of the group leader but represent a unified report to the referral agency.

Family Relationships

Despite abundant profamily rhetoric, many residential programs have long histories of minimizing contact between a youth and his family. Fortunately, this pattern is changing, and the gulf that divided families from their institutionalized children is being removed. Increasingly, parents are being seen as partners in the treatment effort, not as adversaries or patients or targets of blame. Programs like Rosecrance Schools in Rockford, Illinois and Elk Hill Farms in Guchland, Virginia have strong programs for involving parents in support groups, as assistants to staff, and in a myriad of other ways that communicates to parents that "you are important, valued, and we are in this together."

Perhaps one of the most difficult decisions for staff is whether or not a student should have a home visit. The visit should not be viewed as a reward for good behavior; rather, it should be for the purpose of strengthening family relationships, and even at home he is expected to continue working on his problems. Visits of family members to the youth are encouraged even if home visits are not advisable.

Decisions about home visits should be made along the following guidelines.

1. The group believes the student has made enough progress to handle a home visit without hurting himself or others. The group has fully discussed the student's feelings toward his family and has considered both positive and negative results. The group recommends that the visit be granted.
2. The group recommendation then goes to the cottage staff team for a final decision. The staff must be reasonably certain that a student will be able to use a home visit successfully before it gives approval.
3. The local court or referral agency worker has evaluated the situation at home and agrees with the visit.

The essential aim is to prepare students to leave the group, strong enough to withstand most community pressures. The youth who will return to a difficult environment may need a number of home visits to test out his ability to cope with a community placement. Home visits also may be necessary for reasons of illness, accidents, or other catastrophic events, although these should be limited to those that affect the immediate family. Group members and staff should be aware that some students tend to exaggerate marginal situations (e.g., a sick grandmother) to make a home visit appear necessary when in reality it may not be.

As the student approaches the anticipated time of reentry into the community, he should begin to apply what he has learned to the natural setting of home and community. The youth may have to develop associates different from those he had before placement; so he needs enough opportunity to begin shifting friendship patterns to peers who will not reinvolve him in destructive behavior. Since his initial efforts at reintegration may be full of difficulties, the group must keep fully abreast of problems that arise on the visits; hence, close liaison between community, family, and the institution is necessary.

In many settings, students have an opportunity of at least casual contact with parents of members. These contacts can help the group to understand a youth's particular family situation, but the group should not become deeply involved in discussion with other family members. Parents have no basis for trusting the group, and they should not be expected to bring their problems to their adolescent's peer group. Certainly, parents are responsible for working on their problems; changes in the youth accompanied by changes in his parents would be most desirable. However, discussions with the youth peer group do not provide an appropriate context for counseling parents. The literature in the field of family therapy provides rich resources for someone who is planning a program of work with these parents or families who are in need of more specialized treatment.

The Decision for Release

PPC groups are responsible for recommending a student for release when he has sufficiently resolved his problems and no longer needs the group's support. This decision is particularly crucial in residential settings, since the student is terminating placement and moving to a totally different environment. The group must determine whether the youth can function responsibly under a new set of influences.

The youth in PPC is not in a vacuum while he is changing. He is not in a warm, sheltered, temptation-free setting but, rather, in a testing ground for future challenges. He learns why he selected the friends he did and considers the kinds of associations he will pursue in the future. He is exposed to pressures from many sources, and he is confronted with problems of self and others and has periods of trial at home. He succeeds in situations that are ambiguous and hold the possibility for failure.

As the youth returns to the broader peer subculture, he has a clearer understanding of his relationships with peers and adults. He has learned to separate others' problems from his own and is not easily misdirected by negative peer leaders. He is comfortable with many different types of people. His success in helping himself and others has led him toward positive values and a positive self-concept. These changes are carefully observed and evaluated, not only by adults but also by his peers.

In deciding on a recommendation for release, the group must evaluate the individual's behavior and values. As the group has been working very closely with the student, their recommendation is based on broad experience. The recommendation for release should be a unanimous decision, taking into consideration not only how the individual handles himself but also how much he has helped others in his group.

The group possibly could make a poor decision on the release of a member. Perhaps a strong individual is manipulating other members to recommend his release, or a group may recommend the release of a member whom they do not like. Sometimes a group may honestly feel that a student is ready for release, but information available to staff will counter their perception. Regardless, it is still the group's responsibility to recommend any release, and staff then must decide whether to accept or deny the recommendation. If staff determines the group has not made a wise decision, the specific reasons for the denial are communicated to the group. Premature recommendations should be accepted as a matter of course, and staff simply turn the recommendation back to the group for more serious consideration.

The group must be involved in the release process, because if the students feel that despite their work some remote authority controls all aspects of the decision on release, group participation becomes less meaningful. Also, if the staff committee's reasons for turning down a recommendation are arbitrary or insufficient, the group may feel powerless and frustrated, and its motivation may be impaired.

The staff team should anticipate the probability of release early enough to arrange for a smooth transition to the community. Ideally, postrelease planning should begin at the time a student enters the group. The request for release usually will be made after the student has had successful home visits as trials of his ability to operate in the open community. Group members should be encouraged to ask all conceivable questions that bear on this important decision, and the group leader should contribute any pertinent information he may have. In this instance, the leader should not attempt to avoid questions but should honestly and directly contribute his views to the discussion, since the overriding concern is that the group make a proper decision.

The process of thoroughly discussing a request for release generally takes more than one meeting. If the recommendation meeting appears likely to run overtime more than a few minutes, the group should continue the discussion in some future meeting. Release meetings may be held at intervals over a period of several days or weeks until the group has discussed the individual case long enough to make a good decision.

Occasionally, a group will award the meeting to an individual to discuss his release when it is quite obvious that the group is not serious but is handling the whole question flippantly. The group leader has several options in such a situation. In the summary, he can mark the group's lack of concern. Further, if the group attempts to steamroll an illogical recommendation for release, the leader can always rely on the cottage committee to overrule it. The leader also can intervene in the process of the meeting by raising numerous questions that the group must consider in order to make an effective decision.

Some of the important questions that should be answered during release meetings are these.

1. What were the student's problems at home? In the community? In the school? In the group?
2. How has the student shown that he has worked on these problems? Can he give examples?
3. How did the student feel about himself when he entered the group? How does he feel about himself now?
4. What are the student's future plans for school? Employment? Living arrangements?
5. How will the student relate with his family? His peer group?
6. What problems will the student have to face when he leaves the group? How will he handle such difficulties?
7. Will the student maintain some contact with a social worker or counselor? To whom will he go with his problems?

8. What problems have the other group members had and how has the student helped each one? Can he give examples?

9. How have the various group members helped the student with his problems? Can he give examples?

10. Has the student shown care and concern for all members of his group?

After the group has sufficiently discussed the question, each member is asked to give his individual recommendation on whether the student is ready to be released. Although a unanimous decision normally is required, if one member of the group stubbornly attempts to block a release but is unable to give good evidence for his position, the group leader can make an exception to the unanimity requirement.

After the group recommends release, the staff team considers the issue. The decision then is communicated to the group at some time outside a regular meeting so that, should the recommendation be declined, the group can handle any reactions to the decision without disrupting the group meeting. When a release recommendation is approved though, its announcement becomes a significant and highly rewarding occasion in the culture of the group.

Reentry

As the student reenters the community, he leaves the support of the positive peer group and may also lose the opportunity to serve in a positive role. Ideally, the youth would be strong enough to survive amid the pressures of the community. Still, any institutional program certainly must concentrate not only on changing the youth while in residence but also on preparing him for his reintegration into normal community life. To be concerned only with a youth's peformance in the institution is a narrow perspective that has often been referred to as "the unilateral strategy." A sound program also attempts in several ways to modify the social ecology to which the youth must return:

1. Close liaison between institution and community while a youth is in the program.

2. Mobilization of community resources to provide help to the family if feasible and indicated.

3. Careful planning of the youth's postrelease experience, with particular attention to school and employment.

4. Provision of positive peer associations in the community after release.

5. Provision of positive helping roles so the youth can continue to be of service to others after release.

One example of the kinds of innovations possible in a PPC aftercare program is a project in metropolitan Detroit that served youth released from

PPC institutional programs and returned to the community. A dozen former PPC students under the guidance of trained group leaders worked half-time to help all youth returning from residential placement to achieve a successful reintegration into the community. These young people, who work with peers from their own neighborhoods, provide direct services to returning youth and, indeed, benefit themselves, because in salaried positions as "associate group leaders" they have an opportunity to continue serving in positive and productive roles.

NOTES

[1] Richard Babcock and Peter F. Sorenson, "Matching Treatment and Management Systems in Correctional Institutions," in *Managing Human Services*, ed. Jesse F. McClure. (Davis, California: International Dialogue Press, 1979).

[2] Erving Goffman, *Asylums* (Garden City, NY: Doubleday, 1961).

[3] Theodore Palmer, *An Evaluation of Differential Treatment for Delinquents: The Phase II Experiment*, Division of Research, California Youth Authority (Sacramento, Calif., 1969).

[4] Donnell Pappenfort, Dee Kilpatrick, and Robert Roberts, eds., *Child Caring: Social Policy and the Institution* (Chicago: Aldine, 1973).

[5] T. Pfeiffer, "The Use of Physical Restraint by Peers in Group Treatment Programs," (Paper presented at the ninth annual conference, National Association of Peer Group Agencies, Columbus, Ohio, October 13, 1983.)

[6] David Street, Robert D. Vinter, and Charles Perrow, *Organization for Treatment* (New York: The Free Press, 1966).

11

Positive Peer Culture
in School Settings

> So we suggest you sit quietly, behave yourselves, and
> study in the schools we provide as a holding pen
> until we are ready to accept you in the adult world.
> —Harold Howe II

Teachers and principals who daily confront irresponsible behavior among
students frequently come to see the peer subculture as a negative support
system that impairs the teacher/learning process. If PPC in specialized
treatment settings is able to transform highly troubled youngsters into
responsible individuals, then why cannot the public school system as well
benefit from such programs? While positive peer culture to date has a
stronger program based in residential settings than in schools, there is a
growing interest in extending this methodology into the education arena
([5], [6], [9]).

THE DEVELOPMENT OF POSITIVE PEER
CULTURE IN SCHOOLS

Roffers [10] identifies several reasons why PPC can be an appropriate
addition to the school program:

1. The emphasis on responsible behavior is consistent with the school's
   goals.
2. Group sessions can impact on more students than individual counseling.

3. Schools effect a major portion of the life milieu of young people and thus are in a strong position to bring about changes in behavior.
4. The school can create anxiety over irresponsible behavior, thereby demonstrating to a student and his or her peers the need to change these behaviors.
5. The schools can be very reinforcing of positive behavior and provide academic and social success.
6. PPC gives staff a nonpunitive option for dealing with problems indigenous to adolescents.
7. PPC reinforces academic learning since the student with an improved self-concept is better prepared for the risk-taking required to learn.

Transferring PPC methodology from the treatment setting to the public school poses significant challenges, and the literature has not kept pace with rapid expansion of these programs. Roffers [10] notes several key differences between school-based PPC programs and those in residential treatment settings: (1) It is more feasible to create a total climate of caring among those students and staff in a residential setting where all youth are involved in groups. School programs can usually only involve selected students; (2) residential treatment programs are geared to treatment based on the individual's need, and the length of treatment is adjusted accordingly. Public school programs are constrained by the school-day calendar and vacation schedules; (3) residential programs usually have a powerful built-in motivator: release to the community when problems are solved. The extrinsic rewards for successfully completing a school PPC program may be less potent, such as credits on a report card; (4) meeting times in residential settings are usually 90 minutes long and scheduled after school during leisure time. Schools do not have so much flexibility and the program frequently has to be adapted to the existing structure.

Howlett and Boehm [7] have outlined key prerequisites for successful PPC programs in public school settings. Among these are *administrative support* which sanctions the peer group program as a supplement to (not a substitute for) the existing school counseling program and *faculty support* based on a sound orientation to the program, an ongoing communication between group leaders and other faculty. Because of the innovative nature of this program in a school environment, *parental permission* is imperative as are ongoing efforts to communicate with the parents about the program. *Trained leadership* is also a crucial element in successful programs. Schools have trained a variety of personnel as group leaders; most commonly, these include classroom teachers or counselors, but in some settings special education staff and even the school security director have been involved in leading groups.

Roffers [10] proposes a management system for PPC programs in high schools. He suggests that programs in larger school settings should utilize accepted PPC program administrators with skills in both management and public relations. Among the various publics that must be informed and involved are these:

1. *In-school relations*. Concerns of non-PPC staff must be recognized and dealt with. This requires initial informational meetings to martial support and identify areas of concern as well as ongoing informative evaluations of how the program is progressing.
2. *Parental relations*. Both parents of involved students and all other interested parents should be contacted and kept informed of the program. Small groups of staff should be available to meet with groups of parents. Parent–teacher associations, counselors, and social workers can all offer much assistance in setting up parent–PPC staff contact.
3. *Community relations*. School is only one part of the student's world and to the degree possible the concerns of the community at large should be addressed. Businesses where youth may work or shop, recreational or religious organizations, police and correctional agencies, and the general public all are in a potential position to support or sabotage the program.

Roffers also notes that there are important management functions in the administration of a successful PPC program. These include: (1) selection of capable, respected, confident persons for group leading responsibilities; (2) training of staff at preservice levels, either directly or through involving consultants; (3) forming groups using systematic data collection as a basis for selection.

Three different formats for PPC have been employed in public school settings. These are: (1) *PPC leadership groups* composed of both positive and negative peer leaders drawn from all segments of the school; (2) *PPC help groups* composed of students with clearly identified problems interfering with school or personal adjustment; and (3) *PPC classroom groups* made up of students from the same classroom setting. Table 11.1 compares these types of groups. The PPC leadership groups often provide the foundation for the other groups since they impact the entire student culture of a particular school.

POSITIVE PEER CULTURE LEADERSHIP GROUPS

The goal of PPC leadership group programs is to mobilize the indigenous peer leaders in developing a more positive school climate. Since leadership groups are totally voluntary, it becomes important that the school personnel and the group leader in particular be willing to promote the program and secure outstanding candidates. While the idea of "recruiting" youngsters for the program may seem alien to some, the goal is not unlike that in forming an ideal, winning athletic team. In this case, however, the concerns are not

Table 11.1. Formats for School-Based PPC

	Membership	Goals	Process
Leadership groups	Students selected on basis of demonstrated leadership (positive, negative, or mixed) among peers. Membership is voluntary although student may be recruited based on nominations by peers and faculty.	Promote a strong positive culture among leaders of school who will learn how to help others and thereby improve school climate. May assist in establishing "help groups" for other students with special needs.	Initially, building trust and sharing within the group to learn problem-solving skills. Major focus, then, becomes helping other students and working on school-wide problems, such as vandalism. Become a resource to school staff in resolving problems.
Help groups	Students selected because of behavior or attendance problems. Students may be referred by administrative, guidance, or teaching staff or by peers in leadership groups because of identified socioemotional problems.	Resolve behavioral and interpersonal problems of members so they may become positive contributing students in the school. Enhance the self-concept of troubled youth.	Group focuses on problems of its members. Meet daily or several times weekly, preferably at the last period. Group follows similar PPC format as in treatment group. Group recommends to staff that a member no longer has to attend when his/her problems are resolved.
Classroom groups	Students included are enrolled in a common classroom setting; groups are formulated by classroom teacher who serves as group leader. May include leaders, followers, positive students, negative students.	Develop a caring classroom. Resolve problems of members. Teach students positive ways of interacting and helping one another.	Group meetings scheduled on a regular basis or on a need basis. May have features of both leadership and problem-solving groups but is flexibly adapted to the individual class needs.

143

with various athletic abilities but with carefully balancing positive and negative leaders, assertive and quiet personalities, and individuals with various types of interpersonal skills as well as problems. In upper elementary or junior high school groups, it is usually important to place more positive than neutral or negative leaders in groups, because students of different levels of maturity may not be so able to remain independent from the influence of negative leaders. Usually in high school groups, a more even balance of negative and positive leaders is workable. (While we are referring to young people as "negative" or "positive," we in no way mean to label individual students this way. The only point we are trying to make is that public-school PPC programs actively seek out all kinds of youth leaders, however they may be perceived by school faculty.)

Forming Leadership Groups

The Omaha Public Schools program developed by the senior author utilizes the following procedures in forming leadership groups in junior or senior high schools:

1. *Gather student nominations:* Students in classes each receive six index cards. Writing one name per card, they should identify three young men and three young women in their school utilizing these criteria: (a) student they would go to if they had a concern; (b) student they would listen to; (c) student they could trust. Students may say they "don't know," but they should be encouraged to nominate as many as they can.

2. *Gather faculty nominations:* Faculty are asked to complete a simple form identifying nine male and nine female students who are natural leaders in the school (or a given class level for which the program is designed). These are to include positive as well as negative leaders. Note by each name whether positive ($+$), negative ($-$), or both ($\pm$).

3. *Review nominations:* Tallies of nominations by faculty and students are made. Those with several nominations (e.g., 3) form a pool of candidates for leadership groups.

4. *Interview leader candidates:* The group leader or other designated staff individually contact those nominated. The program is explained together with what impact leaders can have. The interviewer builds up students by explaining that they are seen by many as a leader. The students' sophistication and awareness problems in the schools and ability to help others are noted. Students are informed that the groups will be composed of students who care enough and have the strength to make a difference. The program is voluntary—student states whether or not he wants to be involved. They are told that if they are not selected, it is not a put-down.

5. *Select groups:* A PPC committee composed of key school personnel will rank students based on sophistication, strength, maturity, and leadership ability. Groups will need to have a proper balance of positive/negative

students. Racial makeup of groups should be approximately the same as the total school. Close friends or relations are usually separated because of a natural tendency to defend one another. Student and parents are informed of selection, groups are explained to parents, and parental permission is secured.

A major impediment to enrolling leaders in groups is the complexity of scheduling. The student who is taking a full load of courses and is involved in various extracurricular activities does not always have time and may not wish to rearrange priorities for PPC involvement. Some school programs have designed PPC groups into the regular schedule on a daily basis for a semester and granted social studies credit. Other school-based programs have found it is more workable if the group meets two or three times a week over the entire school year. Sometimes, it is possible to schedule groups so that students may attend these during a regularly scheduled study hall. Another impediment is the youth who is harboring some problem (perhaps very private) and is fearful that this might come out in a problem-solving group. While staff might encourage participation, involvement should never be coerced.

The promotion of peer leadership groups in public schools is greatly facilitated by an exclusive focus on learning to give help rather than on needing help. Even in discussing with potential group members their role in problem-solving, the leader must not provide examples of problems that will be seen as "crazy" and thereby threatening to students. Students in any school know peers who are failing, perhaps thinking of dropping out, or who are having problems with teachers or peers. Some students themselves may be aware of much more serious problems (drugs, suicide of youth, etc.), but the leadership groups should not be promoted to youth as targeting of those issues unless they are very widespread in the subculture of the school. This is not to suggest that school-based PPC programs always deal with minor, innocuous problems. In fact, one report of an inner-city high school PPC program [4] described serious problems that were discussed in a girls' group, including shoplifting, auto theft, prostitution, and the sale of drugs.

Leadership Groups in Action

After groups are formed, they typically begin by following a meeting format as described earlier. The initial focus is to teach members of the group communication and problem-solving skills. Unlike treatment groups that continue to look at members' behavior throughout the life of the group, leadership groups, once formed and positively functioning, shift the major focus of group meetings to helping others. Sometimes this involves bringing in another student to meet with the group; in other cases, group members may seek out students who might resist formally coming to the peer leadership group and use a one-to-one or subgroup format for help. As an example, one group member reported that she was working with a friend who had a drug problem but did not wish to bring this to a leadership group. The group provided ongoing indirect help through support and consultation to this helper.

Public school groups are regularly used to assist youth in developing coping skills to meet stressful situations. For example, groups have frequently assisted youth who are dealing with problems of divorce in the family. On occasion, groups have been used to support youth at the time of the death of a parent. One group helped a terminally ill high school student during the months preceding her death.

In reporting on a positive peer culture program in a junior high school a principal highlighted some of the many activities in which the group had been involved, including these: (1) recovering stolen property, including purses, cash, watches and numerous shop tools; (2) effectively confronting peers who behaved inappropriately by harassing and attacking students from opposing schools during a heated basketball game; (3) eliminating restroom vandalism as a leadership group organized a student-operated monitor system; (4) providing support and tutorial assistance to underachieving students who were considering dropping out of school. Because of the status of the members of the leadership group, successful PPC groups may become the "talk of the school." This can further serve to increase spontaneous referral problems to the PPC leadership groups.

A father of a junior high school student called a staff member of the school's PPC program at home on a Sunday morning. He told the group leader that his daughter had been missing since Friday evening but police couldn't locate her and he was desperate. He had heard that there was some kind of group program in his daughter's school, and he wondered if the group would be able to find his daughter. The group leader got the name and description of the girl and called a member of a peer leadership group (one who had a very undistinguished school career in the eyes of school officials). After asking this youth whether he had any ideas about how to locate the missing girl, the youth very willingly replied, "Don't worry about this, Mr. Butts, I'll get back to you as soon as I learn something." By twelve o'clock noon, he had rounded up his friends and involved several high school acquaintances who had transportation available. They began a systematic search of the city. At 6:30 he called the group leader reporting that they had found the girl heavily drugged and waiting on a corner for a pick-up, and they were bringing her home to her parents.*

OTHER FORMATS FOR
SCHOOL-BASED POSITIVE PEER CULTURE

A number of PPC programs have developed in alternative schools where the student population has been separated from the mainstream because of

*K. Butts, personal communication, 1984.

behavior or emotional problems. Certainly PPC can provide a useful methodology in these more "segregated" programs. However, as with a total residential milieu, it would be important that the total organization of the alternative school works to support the group, or a negative result can be expected.

The first school to apply the principles of PPC in an alternative setting was the Bryant YES Center, a Minneapolis inner-city experimental junior high school for approximately 50 students. This "pocket school" served a subpopulation of students who were not succeeding in regular school programs and were provided an alternative academic and group work experience. The program experienced many problems, and at year's end, none of the 22 students who were returning the following year wanted to continue in groups. The basic flow with this program was a lack of organization that led to conflict between group leaders and teachers. A lack of overall faculty and administrative support negated any positive effects the group might have [8]. This experience demonstrated the difficulty of developing a viable program if overall learning environment is devalued by youth.

A number of apparently successful alternative schools for troubled students has been developed around a PPC model. One such program is the Van Wert, Ohio alternative education program, a cooperative venture of the juvenile court, the public school, and a private children's agency [1], [2]. Like many other alternative schools, strong parental involvement was encouraged, and close relationships between students and staff were fostered. The helping relationship was extended beyond the classroom as youth participated in camping trips and extensive community-service activities. Group meetings (but not classes) extended across the summer to assist youth in their adjustment to the community.

Frequently, an individual teacher seeks to develop a methodology for creating a positive group culture within his classroom. One such program is described in detail by Carducci and Carducci [3]. Their book describes ways in which the concepts of positive peer culture can be extended into the classroom environment so as to develop what they have called the *caring classroom*. Rejecting punishment strategies, they describe how a teacher in a self-contained setting can replace the usual classroom control system with a positive group culture. A particularly ingenious innovation in this program is the systematic use of *triads* (subgroups of three students) as the heart of the peer tutorial, behavioral control, and affective education system within the class. The Carduccis outline a procedure for forming these triads and show how the influence of the teacher is expanded as the ability of any individual troublemaker to exert negative influence is curtailed. While other school-based programs are school-wide, this approach allows the teacher to develop a caring classroom even if the school itself is not committed to more pervasive intervention. This will be of particular interest to special educators working with classrooms for troubled youth housed in regular school settings.

Obstacles and Challenges

In interviewing a number of staff connected with school-based PPC programs, we have identified a number of issues and obstacles that are commonly encountered.

1. Most teachers appropriately see themselves as professionals with legitimate authority over the curriculum of the school. Thus, if a peer-group program is imposed on unwilling staff by outside authority, they can be expected to resist this alien force in their midst, thereby reducing the chance of program success.

2. School authorities are sometimes accustomed to denying the existence of problems by sweeping them under the rug. Peer groups, however, are trained to surface and deal with the problems. Until school authorities are assured that the groups will have a positive impact on resolving these problems, they may be reluctant to support the leadership groups.

3. Many school-based groups give credit for participation (usually a social studies elective). While this is an appropriate recognition of the significance of the experience, some teachers may see the students as "rapping" in a class without the usual academic expectation such as tests and written assignments.

4. Counselors can be very supportive of this program, and many counselors make excellent group leaders. However, some counselors, trained exclusively in one-on-one methods, may see the peer group as a threat. Effective programs should seek to develop a good working relationship with the guidance department. In reality, both counselors and groups can maximize their effectiveness if they work cooperatively to improve the school climate. There is also a need for literature on PPC written by or directed at guidance counselors.

5. Teachers who serve as group leaders may experience initial role problems. If they are accustomed to directive or moralizing preachments, this will only shut off group participation. Also, if they have students in both academic classes and groups, they will need to work to keep these separate roles distinct.

6. School officials concerned with efficiency and staffing are often accustomed to class sizes of 30 or more. Unless they understand the principles of small-group dynamics, they may resist allocating staff time to this small a group.

7. Supervisory personnel are unsure of how they should evaluate teachers in leadership groups, since the program does not conform to usual curriculum patterns, and direct observation of groups may compromise confidentiality. Occasionally, the confidentiality of the group may be compromised leading to problems outside the group. For example, a boy in one group pressured his girlfriend to "share" information about his peers. While

abuse of confrontation is not unique to leadership groups, it is an important matter.

8. Because public school groups must come to an end when the period closes, this occasionally means that some problem has been opened but not resolved. If the group leader or some trusted members of the group are not available in the following period, it may be necessary in isolated cases to draw on some other member of the school faculty or counseling staff to assist a student who is not able, at the moment, to reenter the regular school-day program.

9. Without proper direction, programs can gravitate over time from leadership groups to repositories for unmotivated or negative youth. A balance of positive and negative leaders must be maintained if a PPC leadership-group program is to continue as a part of the mainstream of the school environment.

PPC offers a new and promising approach to the problems of America's schools. Too often, educators have been operating under the assumption that the peer group always works to undermine adult authority and encourage misconduct [5]. PPC is geared to neutralize the antiauthority climate in schools by bringing young people into responsible roles within the structure, thereby providing new opportunities for working cooperatively with peers and adults. In the following chapter, we will note recent attempts to evaluate PPC programs in both treatment and educational settings.

NOTES

[1] J. Beard, "The Starr Commonwealth Schools Alternative Education Program," in *Alternative Programs for Disruptive Youth*, ed. by M. A. Thomas, D. A. Sabatino, and R. C. Sarri (Reston, Va: Council for Exceptional Children, 1982), pp. 77–84.

[2] L. Brendtro and M. Mitchell, "Alternative Schools for Troubled Youth: Bridging the Domains of Education and Treatment," in *Perspectives for a New Decade: Education's Responsibility for Seriously Disturbed and Behavior Disordered Children and Youth*, ed. F. H. Wood (Reston, Va: Council for Exceptional Children, 1981), pp. 127–136.

[3] D. J. Carducci and J. B. Carducci, *The Caring Classroom* (Palo Alto, Calif.: Bull Publishing Company, 1984).

[4] J. P. Cronin, "The Effect of Positive Peer Culture on Special Education High School Girls," (Unpublished thesis, St. Cloud State College, St. Cloud, Minn., 1974).

[5] D. L. Duke and A. M. Meckel, *Teacher's Guide to Classroom Management* (New York: Random House, 1984).

[6] H. Garner, "Positive Peer Culture Programs in Schools," in *School Programs for Disruptive Adolescents*, ed. D. J. Safer (Baltimore, Md.: University Park Press, 1982).

[7] F. W. Howlett and R. G. Boehm, *School-Based Delinquency Prevention: The Rock Island Experience* (Austin, Tex.: Justice Systems, Inc., October 1975).

[8] *Jefferson Junior High Pocket School and Positive Peer Culture: An Evaluation,* Minneapolis Public Schools, Minnesota Department of Research and Evaluation, November 1972 (ERIC Document Reproduction Service No. ED 083 311).

[9] W. Kottman, "A School Based Delinquency Prevention Program," (Paper presented at the annual meeting of the American Educational Research Association, New York, March 1982. (ERIC Document Reproduction Service No. ED 219 703).

[10] D. W. Roffers, "The Development of a Model for Implementing the Positive Peer Culture Program in an Inner-City High School" (Ph.D. diss., University of Minnesota, 1975), *Dissertation Abstracts International* 36, pp. 9-A (1976): (University Microfilms No. 7604090).

12

Evaluating
Positive Peer Culture

> Even if evaluation or research does not support fully
> what we are doing, this cannot be seen as a threat,
> for knowledge can only help us improve.
> —Carl Rogers

In recent years, we have seen a renewal of interest in tapping the power of
the peer group in working with troubled youth. A variety of programs have
sprung from diverse treatment philosophies and organizational structures.
Since these methods are still relatively new and developing, it is not
surprising that controversy has surrounded their effectiveness.

A number of authors have suggested caution about claims that peer group
methodology is superior to other approaches. For example, Gold [11]
reviewed research on guided group interaction (GGI) and raised questions
about the effectiveness of GGI in changing attitude, self-concept, or personality. In the absence of unequivocal empirical evidence, Gold counsels
an attitude of skepticism about peer-group approaches. While skepticism
may be an appropriate stance for research, it is a shaky foundation for
practice. The practitioner must maintain a Pygmalion optimism in work with
troubled young people even as the researcher adopts a healthy skepticism or
at times even a cyincal pessimism. However, the researcher who readily
embraces the null hypothesis that "nothing works" fails to respect the
limitations of research methodology and tacitly promotes the belief that
problem youth are incapable of relearning new behavior [34].

It is our observation that many who work closely with PPC programs are
so certain (based on experience or clinical observation) that these

approaches have an impact that they have been less than vigorous in evaluation. When the first edition of *Positive Peer Culture* was published, the authors were also in this position. Understandably, our colleagues were quick to point out that our enthusiasm for PPC was not grounded in formal evaluation or research [12], [24], [30], [36]. Fortunately, however, the process of evaluating positive peer culture is now underway. However, PPC, like many other treatment methodologies, is difficult to properly evaluate because of the complex interaction of several variables. Thus, most criticisms of PPC research are not unique to this methodology but rather reflect the difficulty of evaluating difficult, real world questions.

This chapter reviews evaluative literature on PPC produced during the past decade. While considerable work has been done, it is difficult to retrieve many of these studies. Our efforts to locate existing reports on PPC programs proceeded in this fashion:* (1) A conventional bibliographic search was augmented by computer searches of data bases in the fields of education, psychology, sociology, and criminal justice; (2) a large number of individuals and programs throughout the country were enlisted in the search for possible unpublished reports. The discussion will be limited to programs serving children and youth and to programs identifying themselves (or known to the author) as positive peer culture.

The inclusion of a program in no way endorses such as a "model" of practice (or research methodology), but these are representative of the full range of PPC programs in a variety of school, community, and residential settings. Taken together, they do represent a beginning in extending our understanding of the impact of PPC. The omission of GGI programs from this review is not meant to discredit these efforts but rather to more clearly delimit the focus of discussion.

Since some writers in this field do not make a distinction between GGI and PPC [44], perhaps a brief clarification about our decision to make such a distinction would be useful. Although PPC owes much of its current base of operation and structure to the GGI process developed at Highfields, we believe that PPC programs at this time do in fact have a separate identity. The issue of changing attitudes, values, and self-concept are at the heart of the PPC treatment philosophy. A leading GGI theorist, Frank Petrock [29] acknowledges that research on GGI does not in general show changes in these affective variables. However, Petrock states that such change is not the goal of GGI, which instead seeks to establish self-control over behavior. Roffers [33] identifies other differences between these group models: (a) The focus of PPC is on the total organizational culture, not just the group culture as was the case in traditional GGI programs; (b) PPC places greater emphasis on giving help to others rather than being a recipient of help from the group; the greatest therapy is the process of caring for others; (c) the emphasis is on

---

*The authors gratefully acknowledge the diligent work of our research assistant, Lynn Radke, in locating these resources.

trust and openness rather than coercing members to be honest with the group, and the group should have no sanction to punish or restrict members.

The remainder of this chapter discusses the various studies of positive peer culture that were located in the literature review. These are organized into three major categories: first, the studies of PPC programs in residential treatment settings; second, the somewhat smaller number of studies of programs in school and community-based settings; and, finally practice-oriented and conceptual studies which seek to identify the components of successful PPC programs.

RESIDENTIAL TREATMENT PROGRAMS

Since PPC developed first in these settings, it is not surprising that a growing body of studies addresses the efficacy of PPC in residential treatment. These include affective evaluations (e.g., changes in values, attitudes, and self-concept), behavioral evaluations, and academic evaluations.

Affective Evaluations

Unlike programs that attend only to a narrow observable behavior, positive peer culture strives to influence the attitudes and values of young people and to build a positive self-concept. The relationships between behavioral maladjustment and poor self-concept has been frequently noted in the treatment literature. For example, the delinquent devalues himself and turns outward for control and evaluation on behavior. Data on successful treatment of such youths shows marked changes in self-concept [23]. While there is some disagreement about the degree to which an improved self-concept is a by-product or a cause of improved behavior, there is evidence that the positive self-concept is a necessary (but probably not sufficient) condition in the successful treatment of troubled youth.

The earliest research on the self-concepts of youngsters in PPC treatment is that begun in 1972 by the Michigan Department of Youth Services and reported by Virgil Pinckney and Dale Shears [25]. In the subsequent decade, they collected a mass of data on several thousand youth who had been involved in PPC programs in state training school programs at Adrian and Whitmore Lake. They gathered pre- and posttest data on a 120-item youth opinion poll administered at intake and at release. General findings of this research were:

- *Self esteem.* Youth significantly increased feelings of self worth.

- *Personal responsibility.* Youth significantly increased on a measure of internal focus of responsibility.

- *Delinquent values and attitudes.* Youth significantly reduced delinquent attitudes and values.

Lybarger [20] studied the impact of PPC on male emotionally disturbed delinquents (mean age 14.5 years). Fourteen students were given the Piers–Harris Self-Concept Scale 2 weeks after admission to the program and then 120 days later. Statistically significant increased scores in self-concept were reported over the 120-day period. Lybarger also reported data on two other comparison groups who had been in PPC groups for differing periods of time. When administering the self-concept test 40 days apart (i.e., 54–94 days into program and 94–134 days into program), he found no statistically significant changes in self-concept, although mean scores did improve in each time period. These latter results are to be expected considering the small sample sizes and extremely short period assessed. However, Lybarger seems to misconstrue his own data by concluding that "PPC did not have a significant positive on self-concept until subjects had been in treatment approximately 120 days" [20]. In fact, significant changes did occur in the one group he followed over the major portion of treatment of 120 days.

Wasmund [40] studied self-concept differences between youth at three stages in PPC treatment (new students, students in program more than 1 month, students ready for release). Subjects were 89 adolescent boys (mean age of 15.5 years) placed in PPC programs in either the Minnesota State Training School or Woodland Hills, a private treatment center in Duluth. The Tennessee Self-Concept Scale was administered at each of three stages in treatment, and data were reported on three scales of this instrument. On the "general maladjustment" and "personality disorder" scales, there were statistically significant improvements between new students and those at intermediate or release stages. This trend also held for the third scale, a "total positive scale," but differences were not statistically significant. Also, Wasmund was not able to discriminate differences so clearly between students at stages two and three. He interpreted this to mean that changes in self-concept occur rather early in the course of PPC treatment. It should be noted, however, that this study does not follow the same individuals through various stages of program but rather compares different students grouped by their tenure in the program. Wasmund concluded that students leaving PPC programs in each of the institutions studied were significantly less delinquent and better adjusted than students entering the program.

Wasmund reports two subsequent studies with the Tennessee Self-Concept Scale. Students entering the treatment program were found to score in a manner nearly identical to the Tennessee Self-Concept Scale delinquent norm group [41]. This pattern of delinquent self-concept was consistent across sex, age, and racial categories. After involvement in PPC groups, youth significantly changed in the desired directions (increased self-concept and lower deviant scores) in 13 of 15 measures. The only 2 measures not showing change were "psychosis" and "personality integration" scales where subjects remained at the mean in both pre- and posttest. Noting that even unsuccessful students in PPC make significant gains in self-concept, Wasund attributes this to the existence of a group climate where positive self-concept becomes highly valued. Thus, youth with more severe maladjustment, identity, and family problems score high on a "defensive–positive scale" as they seek to match the gains they see in peers by artificially inflating their self-descriptions. In a final study [42], youth in a Duluth PPC residential treatment program were matched with a comparison group of public school students. At admission, the delinquent youth differed significantly from their "normal" peers on the Tennessee Self-Concept Scale. Specifically, delinquent youth were more conflicted, maladjusted, had lower feelings of worth as a family member, and low regard for social mores or ethics. Tested at reentry to the community, these differences have largely been eliminated and, in many cases, the returning youth scored higher than normal controls.

McKinney et al. [23] administered the Jesness Inventory to boys enrolled in a state training school PPC program. They report a statistically significant reduction in an index of asocial behavior.

Robinson [32] studied both PPC and GGI programs operated by the Michigan Department of Youth Services. Instruments utilized were the Cooper–Smith Self-Esteem Inventory, the Quay Personal Opinion Scale, and the Rotter Internal–External Control Scale. Significant changes included gains in self-concept, decreased negative values and attitudes, and an increase in internal locus of control. Gains in the PPC group were greater in all three measures than in GGI, although there is some indication that GGI groups included some students with more serious-offense histories.

Brannon [2] assessed changes in personality characteristics in a group of 62 delinquent boys enrolled in a Missouri youth center. He utilized pre- and posttests with the Cattel High School Personality Questionnaire. Students leaving the program after an average of 6 months were found to be significantly more responsible, persevering, concerned with moral decisions, more internally restrained, and less frustrated and driven than pretreatment students.

Although the consistency of data on improved self-concept is encouraging, Pinckney and Shears [25] conclude that this variable alone cannot account for the success of youngsters who leave the program. Despite self-concept changes, it appears that the strongest determinant of success (as measured by absence of arrest) is *productivity* after discharge (i.e., either remaining in school or working). While it is reasonable to expect a positive relationship between self-concept and both school success and employment success, it is clear that many variables interact together to determine successful outcomes.

Behavioral Evaluations

One of the most valuable pieces of evaluative information concerns how students fare after they leave a treatment program. However, follow-up and recidivism studies have been plagued with many uncertainties. Is one actually measuring the impact of treatment or the after-care experience itself? Do arrest rates reflect valid measures of youth behavior or are they measures of law enforcement activity? Since populations in various programs are not selected randomly, are they comparable? Despite the many difficulties with follow-up studies, the question of what happens to youngsters after leaving treatment remains a great concern, and several studies of PPC programs address this issue.

The earliest recorded study of PPC was conducted by the Minnesota Department of Correction and involved 729 youth paroled from a Minnesota PPC program [26]. This study claimed a success rate of 81.5%, with recidivism at 18.5% based on parole revocation in a 2-year follow-up. This compared with a recidivism rate of 50% prior to implementation of the program. However, subsequent analysis of the Minnesota study suggests certain problems with the research methodology [35].

Gerrard [10] reports a study comparing parole revocation rates in positive peer culture and behavior modification programs operated by the Nebraska Boys Youth Development Center in Kearney. His results showed a 42.5% parole revocation rate for boys leaving the behavior modification unit and a 14.3% rate for those leaving positive peer culture. The fact that the behavior modification group had been paroled for a longer time limits conclusions that one can draw from these results.

Wasmund [41] reported a recidivism rate of 11% within 90 days after release from PPC residential programs. Using a more stringent measure of success that embodied other indications of maladjustment, he concluded that the failure rate was 23%.

An alternate definition of success was employed by Richardson [31] who computed the percentage of time youth were free from incarceration since having left the institution. This computation produced a "success" rate of about 80%.

Recent data from the Michigan Youth Service program [25] shows that 18% of released students have been arrested for either felony or misdemeanor during the 3-month period following release. They concluded that since nonproductive youth were twice as likely to be arrested and since nearly one-half of youth were nonproductive, there is a strong need for community support systems in the postrelease period.

Nickolaus [28] summarized the research of Murray and Koch which compared the behavior of Illinois juveniles before treatment in various correctional programs with that following treatment. This study included 583 youth who were served by various services, including a typical state training school, residential PPC programs in private settings, camps, Outward Bound, and community and home-based treatment. The question posed by this researcher was not whether delinquency was cured but whether things got better. The effectiveness of various interventions was measured by an "arrest-suppression effect" (i.e., the degree to which the pretreatment baseline for arrests declined after treatment). While all forms of intervention lowered the outcome rate of arrests to some degree (probably an instance of statistical regression toward the means), the most successful intervention was positive peer culture where the arrest rate was reduced by 81.7%. This finding appears to call into question earlier research that generally assumed that group-centered residential approaches, while superior to traditional custodial institutions, were not so effective as community intervention.

A few studies have sought to measure changes in behavior that occur during the course of PPC treatment. Comparing PPC and non-PPC students in a correctional setting, Selection Research [37] evaluated data from behavior rating scales completed by classroom teachers. The data show that PPC students were significantly more positive in areas such as out-of-seat behavior, aggressiveness, completion of assignments, and general attitude toward school and others. Lybarger [19] utilized the Devereaux Adolescent Behavior Rating Scale completed by nonprofessional residence staff in a correctional setting. Ratings were made shortly after the onset of treatment and 120 days later. (As noted earlier, Lybarger had found significant self-concept improvement over this period of time.) Lybarger did not find significant decrease in inappropriate behavior as rated by the Devereaux rating scale, and in one group, negative behavior actually increased. However, these findings would appear to be questionable because of changes in raters: Due to a high staff turnover in the institution, only about 50% of the students had the same staff member rating them at both pretest and posttest.

Taylor and Hepburn [38] sought to compare positive peer culture and token economy programs. Since these treatment philosophies differ considerably, they attempted to develop a research design that would measure each against its own assumptions. While this intriguing procedure merits further investigation, Taylor and Hepburn's study does not appear to yield conclusions that are of immediate practical significance.

Wasmund [40] developed a 24 item Likert-type behavior rating scale that he administered to students in residential PPC programs. A total of 89 students were classified into three comparison groups based on their tenure in the program (less than 1 month, intermediate, at release). Analysis of these ratings showed that behavior was significantly more positive at each successive stage in PPC.

Behavioral incidents observed in PPC were compared with those in a "level system" by Mitchell and Cockrum [27]. These coeducational programs were operated by a Texas residential center, and each served 39 adolescents of comparable intelligence. Researchers coded incident reports into various behavioral categories. Reliability data on the incident reports were not reported. The researchers concluded that in contrast to the level system, the PPC program was much "smoother" and remarkably free of any incidents of aggression against staff. The PPC program reported significantly fewer cases of runaway, physical aggression against staff, property destruction, self-injurious behavior, and "pooled other" behavior. On the other hand, there were significantly more incidents of apparently less severe behavior, including improper display of affection, off-limits, and campus break-ins.

Academic Achievement

Because PPC programs place such a strong emphasis on developing a positive self-concept and because self-concept is known to be closely related to school achievement, one might expect improved school achievement. This is a particular concern in residential treatment settings where it is commonly reported that students enter achieving at levels 2–4 years below their chronological grade expectations. These students bring with them a school history of achieving only one-half to three-quarters a year of academic gain per year of schooling.

Several studies report data on academic achievement of students over the period of time they are involved in PPC programs. The usual research design is to administer an achievement measure shortly after admission and then again at release. Since students are seldom enrolled in residential programs for a standard period of time, such as an academic year, these research studies control for varying lengths of stay by utilizing an index of educational achievement. This index is computed by the formula:

$$\frac{\text{Average gain in educational grade level}}{\text{Average length of stay (days)}} \times 365 = \text{Index of educational achievement}$$

Therefore, an index of 1.0 represents 1 year of gain for each year in program. Four studies utilizing this system were located. Wasmund [41] tested 168 adjudicated delinquents in a coeducational treatment program serving youngsters 13–18 years of age. With a mean age of 15.5, youngsters averaged 2.5 years below grade level academically. He reports a 1.66 grade level equivalent gain per year in program as assessed by the Peabody Individual Achievement Test and the Wide-Range Achievement Test.

Another study [8] reports achievement data on 90 delinquent males aged 10–18 who were enrolled in group programs at the Starr Commonwealth Schools in Michigan. Utilizing the Stanford Achievement Test, these students made 1.50 grade equivalent gains per year in program. Michigan Department of Social Services [25] reports data on 151 delinquent adolescents involved in state training programs for adolescent boys or girls. These students achieved 1.45 grade levels per year in program as measured by the Stanford Achievement Test. Finally Richardson [31] reported a gain of 2.15 years per year in program utilizing the Peabody Individual Achievement Test with 29 students enrolled at Elk Hill Farm in Richmond, Virginia. While these figures are even higher than results reported above, it would appear that this group of students was not fully representative of all youth in the program due to significant attrition in the number who took both the pre- and posttests.

Using a pretest/posttest design, Selection Research [37] compared students in a Nebraska PPC program with non-PPC youth. In this study, both populations were enrolled in a Title I program for the disadvantaged. While both groups made gains, there were no significant difference between groups.

In summary, there is a growing body of research that suggests that PPC programs in residential centers can have a significant impact on altering patterns of school failure and underachievement. Further research will be necessary to determine what the long-range impact of this increased academic performance may be. And it should be noted that although academic achievement is a most worthy value in and of itself, as a single variable, it remains a poor predictor of success [41].

SCHOOL AND COMMUNITY-BASED PROGRAMS

Roffers [33] completed the first major study of the programmatic and administrative issues involved in developing effective PPC programs in school settings. At the time of his study, there was a growing body of practical experience with operating such programs. Although it was not the intent of his research to evaluate PPC, he did report results of a survey of 35 PPC group leaders and supervisors who completed a comprehensive questionnaire on their programs. Respondents agreed that participation in PPC programs led to improvement in class attendance, general behavior and attitudes, and lower crime rates.

PPC programs developed by the Rock Island, Illinois, school system were evaluated in studies over two successive years. One aspect of the initial study [17] was a consumer evaluation questionnaire where participants in PPC rated the program on a 5-point scale. A majority of junior and senior high school respondents indicated "agree" or "strongly agree" that the PPC program: (1) has increased the level of communication among students, (2) has reduced violence (especially fights) in the school, (3) has reduced hatred or racial prejudice, and (4) has helped me to respect the faculty and administration at the school. This study also reported a 40% reduction in truancy, when measured by self-reports as well as by official records. In a subsequent year [1], PPC programs had been extended from the high school and junior high to also include six elementary schools in Rock Island. The programs included both natural leaders as well as problem youth. Pretest–posttest data were reported on 307 students involved in the programs. Conclusions were: (1) The program heavily impacted on delinquent behavior which showed a reduction of over 70% based on self-reports as well as police department reports; (2) self-reported truancy as well as the official records of truancy again declined (34 and 13%, respectively); and (3) disciplinary violation declined but not so much as delinquent behavior and truancy. Hard drug use declined significantly, while use of marijuana was less affected (these effects were more pronounced at the junior high level than the senior high). In their evaluation of the PPC experience, students were strongly favorable about the value of the program, a view generally shared by teachers and parents.

The Omaha public schools in Omaha, Nebraska, have utilized positive peer culture programs to a greater extent and over a more extended period of time than any other school system. The program began in Monroe Junior High in 1973 at a time the school was involved in a desegregation process. Subsequently, the program has been extended to several other junior and senior high schools. Two evaluation reports on Omaha's PPC programs have been completed by Paul Malcolm and Irving Young ([21], [22]) for the research department of the Omaha schools. These data are summarized by Garner [9, p. 326]:

> In 1976, the Omaha Public Schools released Instructional Research Report #9175-10 in which 8th graders ($N=90$) who had participated in the PPC groups were compared with 8th graders ($N=62$) who were not involved in the program. Although statistically significant differences were generally not found, the consistency of the trends listed below is important to note.
>
> 1. PPC students' suspension rates declined after 1 year: 0.31 to 0.26. Control students' suspension rates rose after 1 year, 0.07 to 0.15.
> 2. Tardy rates declined for PPC students from 3.2 to 2.7. Tardy rates rose for control students from 2.4 to 4.3.
> 3. Absence rates rose for both groups of students. For PPC students from 7.5 to 10.3, and for control students from 10.5 to 13.0.
> 4. Grades earned by both groups were almost identical during the 7th and 8th grade.
> 5. Problem-solving abilities stressed in PPC were enhanced by students who participated in the PPC program and were better than those of students who were not involved in the program.
> 6. Attitudes of students toward school for the PPC group remained constant from fall to spring testing.
>
> In 1978, the Omaha Schools published Instructional Research Report #1977-3 which updated the PPC evaluation. In a controlled study of student attitudes, 142 7th and 8th graders who had been PPC participants were compared with a randomly selected control group of 78 students. Students in both groups were enrolled in three different schools. Three measures were administered to both groups including the Attitude Toward School Learning questionnaire, the Attitude Toward School questionnaire, and a situations questionnaire that measured the application of PPC problem solving to hypothetical conflicts. The PPC group scored significantly higher ($P = 0.05$) than the control group on the Attitude Toward School Learning Questionnaire and on the Situations measure. In addition to these measures of attitudinal change, the report cited lower tardy and absence rates for the PPC groups, as well as better grades in reading and mathematics over a 2-year period. The suspension rates were lower for the PPC group in 1976/77 and for the control group in 1977/78.

In assessing the research methodology used in the Omaha studies, Wall
et al. [39] observed that equivalent experimental and comparison groups
were not used. Since assignment to PPC was based on leadership variables
(while comparison group students were randomly drawn from the regular
student body), it is not clear that the leadership group students can be
properly matched with those from the comparison group.

A preliminary evaluation of a coeducational alternative school program
for troubled youth operated by the juvenile court and public schools is
reported by Brendtro and Mitchell [3]. Initial data included eight students
who were enrolled in the initial program an average period of 7.5 months.
Upon entry, the average youth was in eleventh grade with reading and math
achievement over 4 years below grade level. Reading achievement increased from a level of 6.6 at admission to 8.0 at the end of the academic
year as measured by the Woodcock Reading Test. Probably the most
dramatic effects reported were in reducing school truancy. In the year prior
to enrollment in the alternative program, the average youth was reported
absent 25.4% of the days school was in session. In contrast, during their time
in the group program, attendance was 94% with absenteeism at 6%. A
questionnaire directed to parents of students in the program indicated strong
satisfaction with the program in the face of generally negative attitudes
about the regular school program in which their youngster had been
previously involved. Although few conclusions should be drawn from such
a small population of students, these preliminary data clearly suggest that an
alternative school for troubled youth based on peer group methodology can
result in improved attendance, achievement, and attitudes.

Another community-based program serving a population of troubled
youth is described by Cowles [7]. This study compared a group of 37
juveniles participating in a court/public school PPC program in Hannibal,
Missouri, with a matched group of youth also referred to the court but not
involved in the program. The focus was on modifying undesired behavior,
specifically, known law violation. Three measures were taken:

1. *Number of incidents* reported from participants in PPC was significantly greater than controls, although this was probably due to
   increased contact of officers with PPC youth.
2. *Seriousness of offenses* was significantly less for PPC students than
   controls.
3. *Change over time* for PPC youth engaging in less serious behavior
   while reported delinquencies became more serious for non-PPC
   youth.

Summarizing the school and community-based research, it would appear
that although the literature in this area is not so extensive as in residential
settings, findings are generally consistent with the overall positive impact
noted in residential studies. In reading the various research studies summarized in this chapter, the authors frequently wished that they knew more

about the full background of the various programs included under the label "positive peer culture." As Loe [18] has observed, the quality of future research in this area could be greatly improved by more thorough descriptions of program methodology and complete subject and leader data as well as studies of longer duration. However, a more extensive and rigorous program evaluation will be required before one can draw unequivocal conclusions about the impact of PPC in a variety of residential and community settings.

QUALITY CONTROL IN PPC PROGRAMS

While formal program research in *quantitative* evaluation is essential, the operation of effective PPC programs also requires *qualitative* examination that grows from clinical observation, professional expertise, and practice wisdom. We must enhance our understanding of a multitude of practice-related issues such as these:

1. What are the most effective means of staff selection and training?
2. What are the unique problems and opportunities of PPC programs in different organizational settings?
3. What are the common pitfalls encountered in programs espousing this methodology, and how might these be overcome?
4. Once programs are developed, how can they avoid stagnation and entropy and keep flexible and dynamic without compromising the basic underlying philosophy?

In a review of recent PPC literature, we note that many of these matters have been addressed by various authors. In this final section, we highlight several key issues that are germane to maintaining quality control in PPC programs.

This book has outlined a total integrated treatment strategy and cautions against grafting elements of PPC to approaches that are rooted in fundamentally different assumptions (painting spots on the tiger). This is not to suggest that the model is cast in stone and can never be improved. However, one should expect that taking PPC methods out of their context might not yield the most effective results. While the authors are not in a position to evaluate the efficacy of such hybrid extensions of this model, the issue is worthy of mention. For example, one article reports an attempt to integrate positive peer culture with a token economy. Hoghughi [16] describes the program at the Aycliffe School in Darlington, England. He accounts, in great detail, the complexities and problems associated with this approach, particularly in the maintenance of the token economy. In reading this account, one cannot help but wonder whether his attempt does an injustice to both PPC and behavior modification philosophies and whether the program might be better off sticking to one coherent system.

Quality Control in PPC Programs   163

It is widely assumed that effective group programs require effective group leaders. However, our knowledge about the kind of individuals who are best fitted for this task is most tentative. It does appear that the demands of group-leading differ significantly from those of traditional casework or psychotherapy. Wasmund [43] sought to test the "folk concept" that group therapists with delinquent youth possess unique personality characteristics. He administered Cattell's 16 Personality Factor questionnaire to 48 practicing group leaders (69% male, 31% female; 87% Caucasian, 13% black; mean age 30). Compared to available test norms on male social workers, the PPC group leaders were more assertive, enthusiastic, detached, tough-minded, forthright, independent, anxious, harder to fool, and less controlled. Wasmund concluded that the group-leader role best matches those individuals who are insightful, creative, candid, extroverted, and possessing an abundance of tough poise.

The more carefully one conceptualizes practice of a group method, the greater the possibility of evaluating that practice and extending the model into other settings. Thus, practice-oriented literature that helps to specify the programs and procedures unique to a particular setting fills an important need. An example of such a practice manual is the *Iowa Group Work Model* [13] which is directed at staff in group homes and residential treatment centers. These authors discuss a wide range of strategies and techniques of interest to the residential child-care worker in a peer-group setting.

As PPC programs have proliferated, they have been subjected to greater scrutiny. While this has sometimes led to controversy, it has also greatly enhanced our knowledge base about particular pitfalls and problems that can be encountered by misapplication of the methodology. Articles addresssing these issues have helped to clarify appropriate practice as distinguished from mistakes or malpractice. Among the cautions that have been raised by a number of different observers are the following.

1. PPC should be far more supportive than confrontive, but this is not always the case. The use of any hazing techniques, ridicule, or put-down under the guise of confrontation is intolerable and must be prevented [14].

2. Youngsters can make a charade of caring, going through the motions, but not really helping one another. Students may be able to identify the problems of a peer but may not have the skills or motivation for helping, thus leading to frustration [5].

3. Some programs overemphasize training of the group leader but ignore the training of other staff such as teachers or child-care workers [14].

4. A distorted emphasis on confidentiality of the group meeting can serve to build a climate of "group leader superiority" that can interfere with the necessary teamwork relationships among staff [6].

5. Staff can misuse the concepts of *authority* and *unpredictability* by slipping into a kind of gamesmanship and superiority that negates a sincere, responsive, concerned model for human relationships [15].

What are the principle impediments to quality practice of positive peer culture? Brendtro and Ness [4] surveyed staff of 10 PPC programs in a variety of school and residential settings. Their goal was to identify significant problems in the application of this methodology and to propose guidelines for practice. Among the most frequently reported observations by practitioners were:

1. *Abusive confrontation.* Unless staff remain vigilant and monitor the group process, there was a tendency for intense, hostile, verbal interactions to develop. Hostile language and behavior in the guise of helping is an ever-present danger in a population of physically aggressive youth, and clear standards must be set by staff in this regard.

2. *Mechanical communications in problem-solving.* Youngsters may become almost compulsively involved in using problem labels (e.g., "fronting," "authority problem") and though facile with vocabulary, they are not engaged in genuine communication. Excessive mechanical use of terminology, the reversal technique, or other group-oriented jargon unique to an individual program site can interfere with authentic communication.

3. *Family estrangement.* This potential problem exists both in residential and public school programs. The most common problem in residential settings is the existence of elaborate structures to minimize contact or visiting between parents and students (sometimes operating simultaneously with rhetoric suggesting the staff are family-oriented). In community-based programs, there is a tendency for parents to become threatened by the possibility that youth will be carrying information about families into the group situation.

4. *Distant staff relationships.* In some cases, adults use the group as a cop-out for their own involvement with young people, backing off from significant involvement in the life of the group. Some staff are overly concerned with not becoming familiar, but when adults are distant and unable to model positive caring relationships, the group is deprived of this important staff contribution.

5. *Inadequate listening skills.* Although young people rather quickly learn how to confront one another and "preach," they need much more careful training in order to learn to listen and to be sensitive to the nuances of nonverbal and verbal behavior. The group leader is the key person in modeling and teaching this skill to group members.

6. *Staff abuse of control.* This problem seems to occur when staff subvert the focus of the program from helping to control. Once a group culture is established, staff typically find groups more manageable than before. Some staff may seek to conscript the group into service as an enforcer, thereby mutating the caring focus of the program. This appears to be a greater risk in settings with a prior history of coerciveness such as many custodial correctional institutions.

7. *Lack of attention to individual needs.* The challenge in group pro-

grams is to meet the needs of individuals within the group setting. It is essential, however, that staff not lose sight of the fact that the group members are in fact individuals, each with separate needs. Thus, for example, while one student may need to be made more anxious about his behavior, the opposite may be true of another. Like adults, young persons involved in the intensity and stress of group interaction have needs for some unstructured time and privacy. The challenge of balancing the needs of the individual and the group is captured by the Hindu poet, Tagore in *Gitanjali:* "O, grant me my prayer, that I may never lose the touch of the one in the play of the many."

In summary, the practice-based literature suggests several guidelines by which effective programs are measured:

Do staff provide a model of positive relationships? It is a misconception that staff cannot have therapeutic relationships with individual students in a peer-group program. Successful programs are marked by strong, caring bonds between adults and youth. The staff who models aloofness, intimidation, and hostility will be quickly copied by the group. Full staff involvement also entails a willingness to reassert adult authority if the group members are unable to handle problems in a responsible, caring manner.

Are teamwork relationships of adults effective? The optimal program seeks the fullest cooperation of all staff in the organization. Furthermore, every effort must be made to draw the parents of young people into partnership with staff. School programs that ignore parents do so at their peril, and residential programs that attempt to limit family contact undermine the proper role of parents with their children and as members of the treatment team.

Is communication authentic? Any structured system of problem identification, labeling, and resolution is only valuable if it facilitates communication. Staff must ensure that the medium does not become the message. Therapeutic communication must always be genuine, intensely human, and not mechanical. For communication to be effective, youth need skills in listening and understanding equivalent to their ability in confronting.

Are the needs of the individual lost in the focus on the group? No child is the same, no young person responds the same, and no group regimen should be so all-encompassing as to stifle a person's individual interests or relationships. No individual should have inner feelings continually exposed to group confrontation, since everyone deserves periods during which he can be physically and psychologically alone.

Is this a program of peer coercion or peer concern? Giving peers the responsibility for helping carries no authority to employ punitive interventions. Staff must guarantee that attempts to confront youth with the reality of their behavior are carried out in a manner that minimizes the possibility of antagonism by any of the parties involved. Harassment, name-calling, screaming in someone's face, hostile profanity, and physical intimidation have no place in a quality program. Since physical restraint is a restriction of a most basic freedom, it should be used only in *extreme* situations where lack of intervention would lead to greater harm. Programs based on peer coercion instead of peer concern cannot be called positive peer culture.

NOTES

[1] R. G. Boehm, *Peer Group Counseling—A School Based Juvenile Diversion Program* (St. Louis: Gateway Information Systems, 1976).

[2] J. M. Brannon, "The Effects of Positive Peer Culture upon the Personality Characteristics of Incarcerated Adolescents," Paper presented at the Academy of Criminal Justice Sciences, Louisville, Kentucky, 1982.

[3] L. Brendtro and M. Mitchell, "Alternative Schools for Troubled Youth: Bridging the Domains of Education and Treatment," in *Perspectives for a New Decade: Education's Responsibility for Seriously Disturbed and Behavior Disordered Children and Youth*, ed. F. H. Wood (Reston, Va: Council for Exceptional Children, 1981), pp. 127–136.

[4] L. K. Brendtro and A. E. Ness, "Perspectives on Peer Group Treatment: The Use and Abuse of Guided Group Interaction/Positive Peer Culture," *Children and Youth Services Review* 4 (1982): 307–324.

[5] D. J. Carducci, "Positive Peer Culture and Assertiveness Training: Complementary Modalities for Dealing with Disturbed and Disturbing Adolescents in the Classroom," *Behavior Disorders* 5, no. 3 (1980): 156–162.

[6] L. Christensen, "Comment," *Child Care Quarterly*, 5, no. 2 (1976): 121.

[7] E. L. Cowles, "Report on Positive Peer Culture Treatment Program: 10th Judicial Circuit, Hannibal, Missouri," Criminal Justice Program, Northeast Missouri State University, Kirksville, Missouri (undated).

[8] W. Dahms, L. K. Brendtro, and L. Ness, "Where Have We Gone Wrong in Evaluation?" (Unpublished study, 1982, Albion, Mich.: The Starr Commonwealth Schools).

[9] H. Garner, "Positive Peer Culture Programs in Schools," in *School Programs for Disruptive Adolescents*, ed. D. J. Safer (Baltimore, Md.: University Park Press, 1982), p. 326.

[10] J. Gerrard, "An Evaluation of the Positive Peer Culture Program in a Boy's Correctional School" (Masters thesis, University of Nebraska, 1975).

[11] M. Gold, "A Time for Skepticism," *National Council on Crime and Delinquency Journal* (January 1974), pp. 20–24.

[12] A. P. Goldstein, M. Sherman, N. J. Gershaw, R. P. Sprafkin, and B. Glick, "Training Aggressive Adolescents in Prosocial Behavior," *Journal of Youth and Adolescence* 7, no. 1 (1978): 73–92.

[13] A. J. Grasso and J. L. Hoel, "The Iowa Group Work Treatment Model," (Des Moines, Iowa: Iowa Crime Commission, 1982).

[14] C. D. Harstad, "Guided Group Interaction: Positive Peer Culture," *Child Care Quarterly* 5, no. 2 (1976): 109–120.

[15] M. Hoel, "Formation and Techniques of Peer Group Activities," *Federal Probation* 38, no. 4 (1974): 73.

[16] M. Hoghughi, "The Aycliffe Token Economy," *British Journal of Criminology* 4 (1979): 384–399.

[17] F. W. Howlett and R. G. Boehm, *School-Based Delinquency Prevention: The Rock Island Experience* (Austin, Tex.: Justice Systems, Inc., October 1975).

[18] D. C. Loe, "Positive Peer Culture: An Evaluation," Paper presented at the annual convention of the International Council for Exceptional Children, Chicago, April 1976.

[19] W. A. Lybarger, "The Effect of Positive Peer Culture on the Self-Concept and Rate of Exhibition of Inappropriate Behavior of the Emotionally Disturbed Adolescent Male" (Ph.D. diss., St. Louis University, 1976) (University Microfilms No. 762-25-66).

[20] W. A. Lybarger, "Positive Peer Culture—An Alternative Treatment for the Disturber and/or Disturbing Adolescent," Paper presented at the annual convention of the International Council for Exceptional Children, Chicago, April 1976. (ERIC Document Reproduction Service No. ED 122510).

[21] P. J. Malcom and I. C. Young, "Instructional Research Report #1975-10" (Omaha, Neb.: Omaha Public Schools, 1976).

[22] P. J. Malcom and I. C. Young, "Instructional Research Report #1977-3" (Omaha, Neb.: Omaha Public Schools, 1978).

[23] F. McKinney, D. J. Miller, L. Beier, and S. R. Bohannon, "Self-Concept, Delinquency, and Positive Peer Culture," *Criminology* 15, no. 4 (1978): 529–538.

[24] R. G. Meyer, "Positive Peer Culture" (review of *Positive Peer Culture* by H. H. Vorrath and L. K. Brendtro), *Child Welfare* 53, no. 9 (1974): 605–606.

[25] Michigan Department of Social Services, *The Institution Centers: Objectives and Progress* (Lansing, Michigan: Institutional Services Division, O.C.Y.S., 1983).

[26] Minnesota Department of Corrections, *The Red Wing Training School Follow-Up Study* (Minneapolis, Minn.: Research Division, 1973).

[27] J. D. Mitchell and D. L. Cockrum, "Positive Peer Culture and a Level System: A Comparison in an Adolescent Treatment Facility," *Criminal Justice and Behavior* 7, no. 4 (1980).

[28] G. F. Nickolaus, *A Summary of Beyond Probation: Juvenile Corrections and the Chronic Delinquency* (by C. Murray and L. Cox, Jr., Beverly Hills: Sage Publications, 1979). Summary prepared for Missouri Division of Youth Services, July 1980.

[29] F. Petrock, "Guided Group Interaction in Public Schools: Managing Student Behavior through Peer Group Advocacy" (Ph.D. diss., University of Michigan, 1976), *Dissertation Abstracts International* 37, no. 3-B (1976): 1492–1493 (University Microfilms No. 7619214).

[30] E. L. Phillips, "Positive Peer Culture: Charting a New Course for Education and Training with Contemporary Youth" (Review of *Positive Peer Culture* by H. H. Vorrath and L. K. Brendtro), *Behavior Therapy* 6, no. 5 (1975): 717–718.

[31] W. Richardson, *Elk Hill Farm, Inc. Residential Treatment Program Evaluation August 1976 through September 30, 1983* (Goochland, Va.: Elk Hill Farm, Inc., September 1983).

[32] M. J. Robinson, "Outcomes of Two Treatment Technologies at the Michigan Training School for Boys: A Comparative Study" (Ph.D. diss., University of Michigan, 1980), *Dissertation Abstracts International* 41, no. 2-A (1980): 808–809.

[33] D. W. Roffers, "The Development of a Model for Implementing the Positive Peer Culture Program in an Inner-City High School" (Ph.D. diss., University of Minnesota, 1975) (University Microfilms No. 76-4090).

[34] R. R. Ross and P. Gendreau, "Effective Correctional Treatment: Bibliotherapy for Cynics," in *Effective Correctional Treatment*, ed. R. R. Ross and P. Gendreau (Toronto: Butterworth and Company, 1980).

[35] R. Sarri and E. Selo, "Evaluation Process and Outcome in Juvenile Corrections:

A Grim Tale," in *Evaluation of Community Programs,* ed. P. O. Davidson, F. W. Clark, and L. A. Hamerlynch (Champaign, Il.: Research Press, 1974).

[36] C. Schaefer, "The Impact of the Peer Culture in the Residential Treatment of Youth," *Adolescence* 15, no. 60 (1980): 831–843.

[37] Selection Research, Inc., *Positive Peer Culture Program—Youth Development Center, Kearney, Nebraska—End-of-Year Evaluation Study, Summer 1971* (NCJRS Dialog File 21).

[38] C. A. A. Taylor and J. R. Hepburn, *Positive Peer Culture and Token Economy— An Evaluation of the Missouri Division of Youth Services Treatment Programs, February 1977* (NCJRS Dialog File 21).

[39] J. Wall, J. Hawkins, D. Lishner, & M. Fraser, "Positive Peer Culture: Omaha, Nebraska," *Juvenile Delinquency Prevention: A Compendium of 36 Program Models,* Reports of the National Juvenile Justice Assessment Centers, (U.S. Dept. of Justice, March 1981).

[40] W. C. Wasmund, "Behavioral and Self-Conceptual Differences among Delinquents at Two Minnesota Institutions" (Master's thesis, University of Wisconsin–River Falls, 1977).

[41] W. C. Wasmund, *A Research Evaluation November 1977 through March 1980 of the Woodland Hills Residential Treatment Program* (Duluth, Minn.: Woodland Hills, April 1980).

[42] W. C. Wasmund, *The Effects of Positive Peer Culture upon the Self-Concept of Adolescent Offenders* (Duluth, Minn.: Woodland Hills, September, 1980).

[43] W. C. Wasmund, *Personality Characteristics and Estimated Effectiveness of Group Therapists in Adolescent Residential Settings* (Worthington, Ohio: United Methodist Children's Home, August 1983).

[44] J. K. Whittaker, *Caring for Troubled Children* (San Francisco: Jossey-Bass, 1979).

INDEX

Index prepared by Daniel Morgan.